THE LEGACY OF
JESUS

THE LEGACY OF JESUS

His parting words preparing
us for mission today

PHILIP GREENSLADE

CONTENTS

Foreword   7

1. John 12:27–50   9
   Preparing for the Future

2. John 13   27
   The Hospitality of the Cross

   The Legacy of Jesus
   His example
   His commandment

3. John 14   51
   The Journey to the Father's house

   The Legacy of Jesus
   His promise
   His Spirit
   His peace

4. John 15:1–25   83
   The Community of Friends

   The Legacy of Jesus
   His joy

5. John 15:26–16:33   101
   The Advocacy of Truth

   The Legacy of Jesus
   His witnesses

6. John 17   125
   The Trinity of Love

   The Legacy of Jesus
   His prayer

7. **Welcoming the Future**   143

Resources   157
Notes   159

FOREWORD

As always, Lynette Brooks and all the team at CWR deserve credit for seeing another small book of mine into production. I continue to be forever grateful for my wife Mary's patient support. I owe her more than I can say.

I thank my friends Trevor Martin and Stuart Reid for continuing to supply stimulus and refreshment, both of the intellectual and liquid kind!

I am grateful to my colleagues Kathy Overton and, more recently, Rachel Causey, who make my work more efficient and more enjoyable.

In approaching John 13–17, I was aware, even more than I usually am, of how much I owe to keener minds and holier hearts than mine. These chapters are a special country where explorers go unshod and vulnerable as if around a burning bush of revelation.

I am thankful to God that my first teacher of John's Gospel was the renowned New Testament scholar, George Beasley-Murray, Principal of Spurgeon's College during my time there and, later, the author of a well-received commentary on the Gospel.

George's lectures, not least those on John, were unforgettable experiences, an exhilarating blend of passion and deep learning, exact exegesis and enthusiastic proclamation. When he finished speaking, an awed silence usually followed, until we banged our desks in noisy appreciation.

One of my fellow students, who became a good friend, was Bruce Milne. Bruce went on to enjoy a distinguished career as a theological teacher, and author of many books, including a superb study of John's Gospel in IVP's *The Bible Speaks Today Series*. He has lately retired from his post as Senior Pastor of First Baptist Church, Vancouver, Canada.

Both George and Bruce epitomise for me the best of preacher-theologians, truly Johaninne men, 'full of grace and truth'. I was privileged to know them and I am so thankful to God that their lives touched mine so beneficially. I dedicate these reflections to them both.

'And we have seen and testify that the Father has sent his Son to be the Saviour of the world' (1 John 4:14).

CHAPTER ONE

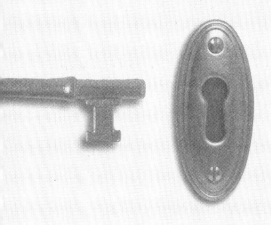

PREPARING FOR THE FUTURE

(John 12:27–50)

PRELUDE

George Smith was a keen art lover.

To fulfil a lifetime's ambition he went one year with his wife to Biarritz to savour the atmosphere of his favourite painter, Picasso, who was rumoured to be staying in a fishing village just down the coast.

Walking on the deserted beach before dinner one evening as the sun sank lower in the sky, George spotted a squat and solitary figure further along the shoreline. As he got closer, he saw that the man, deeply tanned even on his close-shaven head, was drawing fantastic figures in the sand with a discarded ice-cream stick. George ventured closer, still unnoticed by the stooping artist, absorbed in the sweeping gestures of his impromptu masterpiece.

George stood rooted to the spot. Before him was spread a swirling array of Grecian lions, mythical maidens, dancing children strewing flowers along the way. The artist stopped, surprised to see someone so near. He looked at his work and, childlike, shrugged a little sheepishly; then he looked at George and smiled. George could only stare back and whisper the man's name, once, to himself. Then he strode up and down the rows of startling figures, relishing the wonder. His eyes flicked to his hotel window. Should he run and get a camera? But even as he looked, the sun slipped beneath the horizon. The artist smiled again, bid goodnight and was gone.

Later at dinner, as Ray Bradbury tells the tale, George stopped suddenly while reading the menu.

'What's wrong?' asked his wife.

He turned his head and shut his eyes for a moment.

'Listen.'

She listened. 'I don't hear anything,' she said.

'Don't you?'

'No, what is it?'

'Just the tide,' he said, after a while, sitting there, his eyes still shut. '*Just the tide, coming in.*'[1]

Is this how it would be with Jesus?

Here today and gone tomorrow; so lately with us, so soon gone, leaving no trace, no indelible mark on the shoreline of history?

Time like an ever-rolling stream,
Bears all its sons away;
They fly forgotten as a dream
Dies at the opening day.

Isaac Watts

Was Jesus to be no exception to the grim rule?

Jesus wrote in the sand once. What He wrote is not recorded. His words were swept away in a cloud of dust as quickly as they had been written. No trace of them remains.

But that He did write in the ground exemplifies the humble mystery of how our God saves His world. As if God, not wishing to over-ride our will or impinge on our freedom, chooses not to write in unavoidable and intimidating letters in the *sky*. Instead He stoops to write in the *sand*, in the dust of our humanity and

12

our history.

Jesus never penned His autobiography or left His manual of instruction. But if He never wrote a book, He left us witnesses who did.

They were a priceless, indispensable part of His legacy to us.

'This is the disciple who testifies to these things and who wrote them down. We know that his testimony is true' (John 21:24).

> The time of tide shall never
> His covenant remove;
> His name shall stand for ever,
> His changeless name of Love.
> James Montgomery

Let's listen to John and discover afresh the legacy of Jesus.

JOHN 12:27-50

[27]'Now my heart is troubled, and what shall I say? "Father, save me from this hour"? No, it was for this very reason I came to this hour. [28]Father, glorify your name!'

Then a voice came from heaven, 'I have glorified it, and will glorify it again.' [29]The crowd that was there and heard it said it had thundered; others said an angel had spoken to him.

[30]Jesus said, 'This voice was for your benefit, not mine. [31]Now is the time for judgment on this world; now the prince of this world will be driven out. [32]But I, when I am lifted up from the earth, will draw all men to myself.' [33]He said this

to show the kind of death he was going to die.

[34]The crowd spoke up, 'We have heard from the Law that the Christ will remain for ever, so how can you say, "The Son of Man must be lifted up"? Who is this "Son of Man"?'

[35]Then Jesus told them, 'You are going to have the light just a little while longer. Walk while you have the light, before darkness overtakes you. The man who walks in the dark does not know where he is going. [36]Put your trust in the light while you have it, so that you may become sons of light.' When he had finished speaking, Jesus left and hid himself from them.

[37]Even after Jesus had done all these miraculous signs in their presence, they still would not believe in him. [38]This was to fulfil the word of Isaiah the prophet:

'Lord, who has believed our message
    and to whom has the arm of the Lord been
        revealed?'

[39]For this reason they could not believe, because, as Isaiah says elsewhere:

[40]'He has blinded their eyes
    and deadened their hearts,
so they can neither see with their eyes,
    nor understand with their hearts,
    nor turn – and I would heal them.'

[41]Isaiah said this because he saw Jesus' glory and spoke about him.

[42]Yet at the same time many even among the leaders believed in him. But because of the Pharisees they would not confess their faith for fear they would be put out of the synagogue; [43]for they loved praise from men more than praise from God.

[44]Then Jesus cried out, 'When a man believes in me, he does not believe in me only, but in the one who sent me. [45]When he looks at me, he sees the one who sent me. [46]I have come into the world as a light, so that no-one who believes in me should stay in darkness.

[47]'As for the person who hears my words but does not keep them, I do not judge him. For I did not come to judge the world, but to save it. [48]There is a judge for the one who rejects me and does not accept my words; that very word which I spoke will condemn him at the last day. [49]For I did not speak of my own accord, but the Father who sent me commanded me what to say and how to say it. [50]I know that his command leads to eternal life. So whatever I say is just what the Father has told me to say.'

PREPARING FOR THE FUTURE

'Post-Christian' is merely the latest trendy adjective being used to describe our cultural condition in Western Europe after the slow death of Christendom. But if anyone had to face a 'post-Christian' future, it was the first disciples.

The *Farewell Discourses* – as they are called – record the last words of Jesus as He prepares His disciples for His 'going away' and for a future without His physical presence.

The departure speeches of important figures are a familiar feature of ancient literature and practice. This one is particularly reminiscent of Moses' farewell speeches to the children of Israel on the verge of entry to the promised land and there are fascinating echoes of Deuteronomy all through this moving section.

Like Moses, Jesus, too, seals His legacy of teaching with prayer.

But if there are similarities, there is of course a huge contrast between the situation addressed by Moses and that faced by Jesus.

As John Pryor puts it, these farewell words serve 'as more than the parting discourses of a great leader; they fill out the covenant blessings and obligations of the new community of God, as their covenant mediator is about to leave them'.[2]

The second half of John chapter 12 highlights the contrast by vividly setting the scene for the Farewell Discourses of chapters 13–17.

We will put ourselves in a better position to approach the discourses with sensitivity if we briefly explore this setting.

I do this under three headings: *convulsion, crisis, courtroom.*

CONVULSION 12:27–30

'Now is my soul troubled …' (12:27, ESV)

Jesus confesses to being in inner turmoil. The verb used by the evangelist is *'tarrasso'*, suggestive of a turbulent sea, with storm-tossed waves.

Jesus is experiencing violent psychological upheaval.

What John is offering us here, some suggest, is his version of the agony in the Garden of Gethsemane.

But whatever the co-relation with the Synoptic Gospels, Jesus' agitation is real. It echoes His evident distress at the grave of Lazarus (11:33–35), and anticipates His sense of horror over the seeming triumph of evil in Judas (13:21). George Beasley-Murray describes Jesus' state of mind as 'convulsion and shock of spirit'.[3]

Jesus was no plastic man, a cardboard cut-out figure. In Don Carson's words, he 'cannot contemplate the cross as a docetic actor, steeped in dispassionate unconcern'. [4]

Here then are the gut-wrenching, stomach-churning, heart-sickening emotions felt by someone on the verge of battle and so facing imminent danger and possible death. This is our Saviour and Lord. But given who He was and what His mission entailed, He felt these things to an unparalleled degree.

We must never lose sight of the unique pressures bearing down on Jesus, as we see Him – in chapters 13–17 – pre-occupied not with His own foreboding and fate but with the fears and future of His disciples!

At the same time, what we must never do is *pity Him*! Jesus refuses to be spared the pain that, for Him, was woven into the fabric of His destiny. 'What shall I say? "Father, save me from this hour?" But for this purpose I have come to this hour' (v.27b, ESV).

John's narrative has portrayed Jesus with great intensity as moving towards '*His hour*' as something yet to come (2:4; 7:6,8,30;

8:20). But his appointment with God's destiny is now to be kept: 'His hour has come' (12:23; 13:1; 17:1) and He is willing to embrace the turmoil that goes with it.

Characteristically, Jesus brings the burden He bears and lays it on the Father's heart in prayer. And when Jesus prays He has one overriding priority: to glorify the Father's name.

He has taught His disciples just this: 'When you pray, say: "Father, hallowed be your name …"' (Luke 11:2).

Very soon – in the great high-priestly prayer of chapter 17, we will overhear Him praying in exactly the same way: for an honourable vindication of Himself that would bring further glory to the Father!

CRISIS 12:31–36a

'Now' is judgment time for the world and its demonic ruler (v.31).

The word '*krisis*' translated 'judgment' denotes crisis and decision. It is used in conjunction with the word '*krino*' ('to judge'): cf. 3:17–21; 5:22–30; 7:24; 8:16.

Now in the cross the hour of final resolution has come. The world is judged, its false standards of success and power and glory are overthrown.

The final judgment occurs in the cross.

Thankfully it will prove to be a saving judgment.

'In him,' stressed P.T. Forsyth, 'the world passed its judgement on God, and Christ took it. But still more in him, God passed his judgement on the world and Christ took that also.' [5]

We can appreciate the saving judgment of God even more when

we realise that in the cross *the power of evil is defeated* (v.31b). Evil did its worst and lost. Freedom dawns for sin's captives.

The ruler of this world who holds all in his grip is about to be routed and his rule based on falsehood and deception is about to be broken by the truth.

It is in this confidence that Jesus approaches the cross: 'the prince of this world is coming. He has no hold on me' (14:30).

His final words to them as a group are: 'I have told you these things, so that in me you may have peace. In this world you will have trouble. But take heart! I have overcome the world' (16:33).

All this will happen through his being *'lifted up'*.

The idea of 'lifting up' is elsewhere associated with Christ's ascension and exaltation to glory (cf. Acts 2:33; Phil. 2:9).

The terminology of 'lifting up' (*'hupsothenai'*) probably echoes the Greek text of Isaiah 52:13 (LXX, the Greek version of the Old Testament) where it is used to introduce the suffering of the servant.

This may be the clue that John develops in making his unique and profound contribution to the New Testament understanding of the cross.

For John the elevation to glory is directly brought into association with the cross! The ambiguity of language helps to fuse these two things into a stunning paradox: being lifted up from the ground on the cross of crucifixion is itself the exaltation of Jesus from humiliation to glory!

'"But I, when I am lifted up from the earth, will draw all men to myself." He said this to show the kind of death he was going to die' (12:32–33). *The 'lifting up' of Jesus on the cross is paradoxically Jesus' lifting up in glory!*

'Now' is the time of glorification for the Son and therefore for the Father (12:23; 13:31).

The 'lifting up' from the earth in glory matches the 'falling into the ground' in humiliation and death!

Earlier, the Greeks had asked to see Jesus (12:21): the question arises, *when* will they see Him? The answer is a paradoxical one: they will truly see Him for who He really is only when He is obscured from sight – like a seed being buried – in His shameful death.

It is as we look at the cross that 'we behold his glory'.

It is the cross that will prove the *magnet that draws all men – Greeks among them – to Him*. He will draw 'all men' means 'all men' without distinction, not 'all men' without exception.

It is chiefly by being the dying Saviour that He will exercise universal authority and by the compulsion of sacrificial love that He will attract people from every nation under heaven, ironically confirming the worst fears of the Pharisees that 'the whole world has gone after him!' (12:19).

For the moment, 'no one believes our report'. But what even the uplifted voice of Jesus did not do, His uplifted cross will do! Meanwhile the light shines in the darkness.

The hour of decision has struck: 'While you have the light, believe in the light …' (12:36a, ESV).

'Though he had done so many signs before them, they still did not believe in him …' (12:37, ESV).

Though, perhaps with his intended readership's current

struggles with the synagogue in mind, the evangelist notes that a number of Jewish leaders secretly believed in Jesus (12:42).

For the most part, however – as the prologue made clear – 'he came to his own, and his own people did not receive him' (1:11, ESV).

Finding scriptural precedent for this, John makes the connections with Isaiah (12:37–43).

Jesus faces rejection (v.38: 'who has believed our report …', NKJV). But in the prophetic perspective, even this lies within the sovereign purpose of God ('they could not believe, because …' v.39).

What comes into view in Jesus fulfils the long-range vision of the prophets; His glory is the glory of God that flooded their hearts and filled their vision (v.41).

Reflecting upon Isaiah 52–53 we may well conclude that Isaiah in his own way did see deeper and further than anyone among the prophets, the very glory of the Messiah (v.41)!

The tragic irony is that the pagan Greeks want to see Him but His own people refuse to see Him! Even more ironically, their refusal only confirms His rightful place at the climax of their story as the prophet Isaiah had foreseen (12:38/Isa. 53:1; 12:40/ Isa. 6:10).

Sadly, a self-interested quest for popularity prevented even those leaders sympathetic to Jesus from publicly espousing His cause (v.42).

The implication is clear: the judgment, in the cross, of the world and its ruler, on which hangs the destiny of all humanity, constitutes also the *ultimate crisis for Israel*.

COURTROOM 12:36b–50

The judgment on the world and its value system; the expulsion of the reigning powers of evil; the exaltation – contrary to all expectations – of the humiliated and crucified One; the exposure of those who purport to seek God's glory when in fact they serve their own – all this amounts to *a great reversal*.

The verdict on Jesus in the court of human opinion is decisively overturned by a higher authority.

In the light of this impending 'great reversal', everything Jesus says becomes a moment of judgment (vv.47–50).

Throughout the Gospel Jesus is presented – with a great deal of irony – as *on trial*.[6] The Old Testament root of this scenario is painted in Isaiah 40–55 where, through a lawsuit issued by the prophet, Yahweh summons the pagan gods and their worshippers to a trial to settle who is the true God.

In this cosmic courtroom, God looks to Israel to be His 'witnesses' to give testimony on His behalf and to identify Him as the One true God.

Selected examples of this message will suffice.

Isaiah 41:1–4
Does the exile to Babylon show the superiority of the Babylonian deities? This is the question first put to the court. A legal contest ensues to determine the identity of the One true God.

Isaiah 41:21–29
Through the prophet, Yahweh challenges the nations to set forth their case and bring their evidence.

In fact, Yahweh had both forewarned of the exile and has 'stirred up' one who will bring about Babylon's demise (v.25). What else can be said but that Yahweh is 'right' (v.26b)?

Isaiah 43:8–13

The lawsuit is pressed home with the challenge to Israel to stand up and be counted as Yahweh's 'witnesses' (vv.9b–10).

God adds His own testimony as co-witness since in Deuteronomic law, the testimony of two witnesses is required for truth to be established (v.12).

Isaiah 44:6–8

Here God invites anyone who challenges Him to stand up in court and, when no one responds, He turns to Israel again.

Isaiah 45:18–25

God is introduced as the One Creator God, the One who alone can say, 'I am the LORD, and there is no other' (v.18b; cf. 41:4; 44:6; 48:11–12).

The issue of truth; the 'I am' sayings; believers as God's witnesses; the honour of His name: the theme of glory – these surely are among the key biblical building blocks for John's vision of Jesus.

This trial motif then, echoing Isaiah – as Andrew Lincoln so ably shows – is a prominent feature of John's Gospel.

Now, the indictment is that Israel has failed in her task to be God's witnesses, bearing testimony to the world about the truth of the one true God. But where Israel fails, the one true Israelite, Jesus, comes – as He reminds Pilate at the climax of the trial – to 'bear witness to the truth' (18:37–38).

Jesus is the faithful witness.

His accusers, the Jews, are tragically and ironically siding with the pagan worshippers in setting themselves against Jesus and so failing to acknowledge the truth of God incarnate in Him.

The One Creator God – as in Isaiah – re-asserts His right, as Judge, to summon the world to a lawsuit.

Jesus is identified in John's vision with the 'logos' who shares in the creative supremacy of God and is the self-expression of God. So Jesus is One 'sent' by the Father as His authorised agent to press God's case.

So close is the relationship between God and Jesus, Father and Son, that our response to, and treatment of, the latter is considered to be a response to, and treatment of, the former (eg 12:44–45; cf. 5:23; 15:23)!

So Jesus stands in for God as Judge, just as He stands in for Israel as witness!

The conflict He faces with the Israel of His day represents or encapsulates God's conflict with the world. But the mission on which He has been sent has – as its aim – not condemnation but salvation (3:17). As we are reminded here on the verge of the Farewell Discourses – He has not to come to 'judge the world, but to save it' (12:47).

As we saw earlier, this severe but saving judgment is about to have its critical moment in the lifting up of Jesus in the hidden glory of the cross (12:31–32).

24

From John's angle of vision, in A.M. Ramsey's words, 'Calvary is no disaster which needs the Resurrection to reverse it, but a victory so signal that the resurrection follows quickly to seal it.'[7]

And, we might add, it is a triumph so unlikely, and buried so deep in the obscurity of shameful death, that *only* resurrection will make its victory visible!

His claim to truth is vindicated ironically by the very event in which the world passes its judgment on Him; a verdict the resurrection shows to have been overturned and reversed by God Himself. The trial in this decisive sense is over.

What the Farewell Discourses show, however, is that, in another important sense, the trial is not over at all. Jesus remains on trial throughout subsequent history and with Him the God whom He incarnates.

As Andrew Lincoln has it, 'In John 13–17 it emerges that the disciples are to be Jesus' successors in the trial, and the grounding is provided for their future role.'[8]

His followers are now called to be His *witnesses* and empowered to be so by the Holy Spirit whom He sends to them from the Father.

In fact the disciples and the Holy Spirit will bear *joint-witness* to the truth of who Jesus is. In the cosmic courtroom, the Spirit acts as *advocate*. In turn, He is the *prosecuting counsel* who convicts the world of sin, righteousness and judgment; and the *counsel for the defence* who comes alongside the disciples of Jesus to support and strengthen them as they give their testimony to the truth in the extended trial before a sceptical world.

So John 12:36–50 effectively summarises the first half of the

Gospel in which Jesus has exercised a *public* ministry. Now for a while (v.36b) He '*hides Himself*' from public gaze in the *private* company of His disciples (chap. 13–17).

CHAPTER TWO

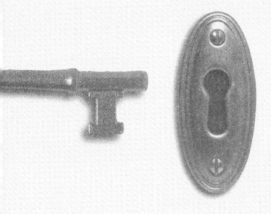

THE HOSPITALITY
OF THE CROSS

(John 13)

The Legacy of Jesus

His example
His commandment

JOHN 13

¹It was just before the Passover Feast. Jesus knew that the time had come for him to leave this world and go to the Father. Having loved his own who were in the world, he now showed them the full extent of his love.

²The evening meal was being served, and the devil had already prompted Judas Iscariot, son of Simon, to betray Jesus. ³Jesus knew that the Father had put all things under his power, and that he had come from God and was returning to God; ⁴so he got up from the meal, took off his outer clothing, and wrapped a towel round his waist. ⁵After that, he poured water into a basin and began to wash his disciples' feet, drying them with the towel that was wrapped round him.

⁶He came to Simon Peter, who said to him, 'Lord, are you going to wash my feet?'

⁷Jesus replied, 'You do not realise now what I am doing, but later you will understand.'

⁸'No,' said Peter, 'you shall never wash my feet.'

Jesus answered, 'Unless I wash you, you have no part with me.'

⁹'Then, Lord,' Simon Peter replied, 'not just my feet but my hands and my head as well!'

¹⁰Jesus answered, 'A person who has had a bath needs only to wash his feet; his whole body is clean. And you are clean, though not every one of you.' ¹¹For he knew who was going to betray him, and that was why he said not every one was clean.

[12]When he had finished washing their feet, he put on his clothes and returned to his place. 'Do you understand what I have done for you?' he asked them. [13]'You call me "Teacher" and "Lord," and rightly so, for that is what I am. [14]Now that I, your Lord and Teacher, have washed your feet, you also should wash one another's feet. [15]I have set you an example that you should do as I have done for you. [16]I tell you the truth, no servant is greater than his master, nor is a messenger greater than the one who sent him. [17]Now that you know these things, you will be blessed if you do them.

[18]'I am not referring to all of you; I know those I have chosen. But this is to fulfil the scripture: "He who shares my bread has lifted up his heel against me."

[19]'I am telling you now before it happens, so that when it does happen you will believe that I am He. [20]I tell you the truth, whoever accepts anyone I send accepts me; and whoever accepts me accepts the one who sent me.'

[21]After he had said this, Jesus was troubled in spirit and testified, 'I tell you the truth, one of you is going to betray me.'

[22]His disciples stared at one another, at a loss to know which of them he meant. [23]One of them, the disciple whom Jesus loved, was reclining next to him. [24]Simon Peter motioned to this disciple and said, 'Ask him which one he means.'

[25]Leaning back against Jesus, he asked him, 'Lord, who is it?'

[26]Jesus answered, 'It is the one to whom I will give this piece of bread when I have dipped it in the dish.' Then, dipping the piece of bread, he gave it to Judas Iscariot, son of Simon. [27]As soon as Judas took the bread, Satan entered into him.

'What you are about to do, do quickly,' Jesus told him, [28]but no-one at the meal understood why Jesus said this to him. [29]Since Judas had charge of the money, some thought Jesus was telling him to buy what was needed for the Feast, or to give something to the poor. [30]As soon as Judas had taken the bread, he went out. And it was night.

[31]When he was gone, Jesus said, 'Now is the Son of Man glorified and God is glorified in him. [32]If God is glorified in him, God will glorify the Son in himself, and will glorify him at once.

[33]'My children, I will be with you only a little longer. You will look for me, and just as I told the Jews, so I tell you now: Where I am going, you cannot come.

[34]'A new command I give you: Love one another. As I have loved you, so you must love one another. [35]By this all men will know that you are my disciples, if you love one another.'

[36]Simon Peter asked him, 'Lord, where are you going?'

Jesus replied, 'Where I am going, you cannot follow now, but you will follow later.'

[37]Peter asked, 'Lord, why can't I follow you now? I will lay down my life for you.'

³⁸Then Jesus answered, 'Will you really lay down your life for me? I tell you the truth, before the cock crows, you will disown me three times!'

The dirt roads of the Middle East and the open sandals worn by travellers made foot-washing a necessity if you were to enter the house as a guest. But this was menial work, a job fit only for a slave at the bottom of the pecking order.

And Jesus does it for His disciples.

Removing His outer cloak, Jesus takes a basin of water and a towel and kneels to wash their dusty feet.

It is a stunning and even scandalous inversion of custom, an act of provocative condescension. It is an unforgettable image, leaving an indelible impression on Christian artists and artisans alike ever since.

What Jesus does is made more memorable and meaningful by the context in which it is set.

The time setting is not accidental: 'Now before the Feast of the Passover …' (13:1, ESV). His impending death on the cross will thoroughly and completely bring into effective reality all that was intended by the Passover ritual to deal with human sin.

Anthony Kelly and Francis Moloney summarise well: 'In the now of the decisive hour, all previous celebrations lead to this crucial Passover in which the generative love of the Father will be disclosed. As Jesus passes out of this world to the Father, he brings to fulfilment the movement that the Exodus of Israel pre-figured.'[1]

That the foot-washing parable took place *before* the Passover Feast may also indicate that His atoning death will for ever pre-empt all *future* Passovers.

The cross will come to be seen as God's full and final provision for the atonement of our sins.

Furthermore, Jesus knew that 'his hour' had come ... (13:1).

John's narrative – as we mentioned earlier – has portrayed Jesus with great intensity moving towards 'his hour' as something yet to come (2:4; 7:6,8,30; 8:20). But His appointment with God's destiny is now to be kept: His hour has come (12:23; 13:1; 17:1) and He is willing to embrace it. His 'hour' is God's hour too.

All prophetic paths lead here to this point.

Now is the climax of God's redemptive purpose towards which God's mysterious working in history has been moving; on this 'hour' all previous promises and covenantal commitments are converging.

The long saving story reaches its critical moment.

God's sovereignty is therefore not taken by surprise by the turn of events. Events that unfold in a seemingly anarchic way are still within the parameters of God's sovereign will.

So even the deadly disloyalty of one of His own followers fulfils the scriptural expectations (v.18b) and Jesus knows who it is who will 'betray him' (v.11).

The events which now begin to unfold will come to be seen as the decisive 'hour' of God's sovereignty.

And notice the personal significance of what is happening, spelt out for us by John in these moving words, '... *having loved his own ... he loved them to the end'* (13:1, ESV). The drama which is now reaching its climax will show the full extent of His love for His disciples.

- Here is love beyond measure; love beyond limits; love to the uttermost; love that never ceases, never fails.
- Here is love vast as the ocean; love that will not be quenched by the waters of death.
- Here is love so penetrating that it will flush out evil from the last grubby and furtive recesses of the heart of Judas; love that even then can't stop itself – in love's last appeal – from offering the broken bread of covenant to the arch-covenant breaker!
- Here is God's love burning like a fire in Jesus that will stop at nothing to achieve its '*telos*' or goal; love that will pay any price at its own expense to win back God's creation.

This is the love of God in Jesus that will not relent until it can cry 'It is finished' (19:30); love that meanwhile demonstrates the lengths to which it will go as it stoops to conquer.

Given the momentous events now unfolding, it is all the more remarkable that Jesus takes time to wash feet. And think of what is going on in Jesus' mind at this very moment as John recalls it.

Reflect on His *self-knowledge*. '… Jesus knew that his hour had come to depart out of this world to the Father …' (13:1), and He knew 'that the Father had given all things into his hands, and that he had come from God and was going back to God …' (13:3).

This is a level of self-awareness that makes His willingness to wash their feet all the more striking.

For Jesus, the cross is self-consciously at the heart of His mission. The cross will be no accident. It is the culmination of Jesus' own awareness of His origin and destiny. He deliberately embraces the cross as in His Father's will and as the gateway back to the Father. The foot-washing is a deeply moving sign of this.

That Jesus has full knowledge of all the Father has entrusted to Him – authority over all flesh to bestow eternal life (v.17) – enhances the wonder of what He does.

With a deepening sense of who He really is, of His glorious origins and future with the Father … knowing *all this*, He does not stand on His dignity; to use Pauline language, He does not seek to exploit His status as the Lord of glory or attempt to turn it to His own advantage but, as a servant, bends to clean their dirty feet!

Given the extraordinary scale of the story in which Jesus knows Himself to be the crucial chapter, it is all the more remarkable that He is concerned not with His own majesty or destiny but with the mundane needs of His disciples and the mundane duty of serving them

What is Jesus doing?

Jesus Himself concedes that only *afterwards* – after the resurrection – will the disciples begin to understand why He did it (13:7).

From the privileged post-Easter vantage-point we share with John we can see that the foot-washing has two main features: it is a *symbolic enactment and a supreme example.*

It is, first of all,

(A) A SYMBOLIC ENACTMENT 13:1–11

In Bruce Milne's words, 'With the hindsight of the cross, we can appreciate what Jesus is doing ... He is performing a symbolic pre-figuration of his cleansing sacrifice at Calvary.'[2]

The very verbs used here for 'taking off' or 'laying down' His outer garments and for 'taking up' or 'putting on' His clothes again (13:4,12) are the same verbs used earlier when He spoke of 'laying down' His life and 'taking it up again' (10:17–18).

As Craig Koester says, 'by removing his clothing, Jesus heightens the sense of scandalous self-giving conveyed by the footwashing and anticipates his final act of self-giving in the death by crucifixion.'[3]

Viewed in this way as an acted parable, the foot-washing anticipates a number of vital aspects of the death of Christ.

Foot-washing was service rendered to those coming to stay in your house. And so we may speak in particular – as a number of theologians are doing – of the *'hospitality of the cross'*.

In his study of the atonement, Hans Boersma writes of God's work of reconciliation in Jesus Christ as 'an expression of God's hospitality toward us'.[4]

Jonathan Wilson suggests that 'hospitality is at the very heart of the gospel. In that gospel Jesus Christ comes to us and gives himself in death so that we may be welcomed into God's family'.[5]

The hospitality offered by His death on the cross involves at least two things: *washing and welcome.*

The cross *washes* us clean

'A conventional ritual,' says Craig Koester, 'points to cleansing

THE HOSPITALITY OF THE CROSS

of another order.'[6] When Peter protests at what Jesus is doing, Jesus replies: 'If I do not wash you, you have no share with me' (13:8, ESV).

His coming death on the cross, Jesus implies, will wash us clean from a deeper defilement than dirt – the defilement of sin. Once this deep cleansing has taken place in us, we will need only daily renewal in the good of it to keep us clean from the contamination of living in a sinful world.

'The one who has bathed does not need to wash, except for his feet, but is completely clean' (13:10, ESV). This is no magical or mystical experience, for up to this point His word has kept them clean (15:3). So in future it will be the believing re-application of the Word or atoning truth of the cross that will wash away our sins and keep us clean along the way.

The cross *welcomes* us home

Foot-washing is an act of loving welcome and inclusion. Beyond the initial grace lies the inviting prospect of feasting and conversation and fellowship.

Our sins washed away, and reconciled to God, we are invited by the hospitality of the cross to enter and enjoy the presence of the Father who, Jesus says, comes to make His home with us (14:23).

Andrew Lincoln sees this as characteristic of John's view of the cross. 'In the Fourth Gospel, God's saving judgment on behalf of humanity can be seen as an act of hospitality that takes place in the face of human inhospitality towards God.'

'God's welcoming love,' he goes on to say, 'is such that, in the gift of the Son, God suffers humanity's violence in order to make space within God's self for this hostile other by sharing the divine life …'[7]

All this anticipates the eternal 'homecoming' which Jesus is going to make ready for us.

The Father, say Kelly and Moloney, is the 'Paternal Host'. 'The spaciousness of the Father's house,' they suggest, 'into which Jesus is going to prepare a place for those who follow him, already breathes an overwhelming hospitality.'[8]

The cross is the unique welcoming threshold for repentant sinners crossing over to be embraced by grace.

'It is in the Cross,' says Boersma, 'perhaps more than anywhere else, that we see the face of the divine host: the true love of God.'[9]

The second feature of the foot-washing underlined by Jesus Himself is that it is:

(B) A SUPREME EXAMPLE 13:12–17

'Now that I, your Lord and Teacher, have washed your feet, you also should wash one another's feet. I have set you an *example* that you should do as I have done for you' (13:14–15, my italics).

'Do as I have done' is not meant to be taken with wooden literalness, at least, not exclusively so.

There is of course an honourable history of Christian groups, mainly in the Peace tradition, who faithfully practise literal washing of feet. Anyone who has ever been involved in such an act – whether giving or receiving – is scarcely unmoved by it; many would testify to it being a deeply humbling experience.

But if not to be taken literally, then the command must be taken seriously as our law of life; the creation among us of all that the foot-washing symbolises: *hospitality, acceptance, inclusion* and *embrace*.

This is the legacy of Jesus: He leaves us His example.

Only afterwards will any of us understand this legacy. A post-Easter understanding will grasp that the cross means the washing away of sins, and welcome to the Father's house. Equally, it will begin to feel the full force of this acted parable of Jesus in shaping attitudes and relationships in the Church.

In the light of the resurrection and Pentecost, we may realise, in Michael Gorman's words, 'that the nonretaliatory, hospitable, cruciform love of God in Christ is paradigmatic for the Christian community in both its external and internal affairs'.[10]

That is, we are to welcome one another within the Body of Christ and be prepared to welcome strangers.

The love of God in the cross of Christ does not reach its desired end until it has created a cruciform community that is its true sequel.

'The practice of hospitality,' says Reinhard Hutter, 'is, therefore, both a reflection and extension of God's own hospitality – God's sharing of the love of the triune life with those who are dust.'[11]

If we risk, for a moment, looking at Jesus' action from a psychological point of view, we might suggest that the secret of Jesus' astonishing humility lies in His sense of total security about who He is. Secure in the knowledge of His origin ('that He had come from God'), His destiny ('and was returning to God'), and His God-given authority ('the Father had put all things under His power'), He could, without embarrassment or loss of face, bend to wash His disciples' feet. Being free from the incessant demand to prove Himself, free from the pressure to keep up appearances, allowed Him without artifice or self-denigration to stoop low in humility and service.

Perhaps, to some degree, the same is true for us. The more secure we are, in Christ, in being washed and welcomed and loved to the uttermost by the Father, the less self-protective we may dare to be.

We will have to die to self to reach this point. Hospitality is no more natural to us than washing feet. In Jonathan Wilson's words, 'The crucifixion was the ultimate act of our hostility – we crucified our host, the very source of our life. This teaches us that to practice hospitality we must be changed.'[12]

We must, as Henri Nouwen put it, make the movement from hostility to hospitality.[13] Only the hospitality of the cross can create the 'hospitality of the heart' – to use David Ford's vivid phrase.[14]

Only 'in Christ' can we be set free from the destructive insecurity that makes us either over-assert ourselves against our neighbour or demean ourselves in self-loathing. Humility is possible to those whose lives have been re-rooted in the love of God in Christ. Humility is the fruit of lives which have died to self and come alive in Him. Humility suits those who are sourced by the same fatherly love as Jesus and who, in Him, know where they too are going. If my past and future and my present times are in God's hands, then it does not devalue me to take a towel and wash feet. As the master, so the servant. Such is the blessed life.

In that original Upper Room, were the disciples embarrassed to death, shamed by grace? Should they not have pre-empted Him by spotting the need before He did? Maybe, though there is no clear word of reproach.

What matters is a lesson learned. Call him Teacher and Lord as we are right to do. But if we do then we are called to follow His lead in humble service of one another. After all no servant is greater than his master; and He remains Master and Lord.

So, as we used to sing:

> Put on the apron of humility
> Serve your brother, wash his feet
> That he may walk in the way of the Lord,
> Refreshed, refreshed ...

We often balk at face-to-face encounters, how much more face-to-*feet* meetings?

As Douglas Webster well says: 'It is a terrible irony when Christians excuse their failure to become like Jesus by using the docetic excuse that his deity makes him exceptional.'[15]

In fact because, uniquely, He humbled Himself to death to save us, everything about Him is relevant to our lives. His story is to be our story as through the cross we die to sin and begin to live out of the Christ-life.

Only those can bend to wash each other's feet who have been washed by the sin-cleansing love of Calvary. Empowered by the Spirit, our actions will flow from the self-giving love of the cross.

That eloquent Methodist of a previous generation, A.E. Whitham, once told of a dream in which he had toured the Museum of Heaven.

> ... I saw a widow's mite and the feather of a small bird ... swaddling clothes, a hammer and three nails ... a bit of a fishing net, and the broken oar of a boat. I saw a sponge that had once been dipped in vinegar, and a small piece of silver. While I was turning over a common drinking cup which had a very honourable place, I whispered to the attendant, 'Have you got a towel and a basin among your collection?' 'No,' he said, 'not here: you see *they are in constant use*'!

'Then,' said Whitham, 'I knew I was in heaven!'

Jesus expects every believer to do his or her duty and so 'wash one another's feet' that a foretaste of heaven may be savoured on earth. 'If you know these things, blessed are you if you do them!'

To that end, may the cleansing grace of the Lord Jesus Christ, the welcoming love of God and the hospitality of the Holy Spirit, be with us all, Amen.

(C) A SEARCHING EXPOSURE 13:18–38

The events that are now unfolding which lead to the cross will bring out the best and worst in us.

The approaching trial will expose the fault lines that run through a facile discipleship and will bring to the surface the hidden agendas of corrupted hearts.

Hospitality as rich and royal as that symbolised by the foot-washing is not an easy option; nor is it indiscriminate. Here 'reality is harsh to the feet of shadows'. No one can attempt to cross the threshold of the Father's holy love and hope to remain unchallenged or unchanged.

All who are stained by sin, dishevelled from the futile travelling in their own strength, the humble and needy, are washed and made welcome. But those bent on betrayal face exposure (cf. John 3:20). Jesus expects it (13:18a). Even in this case, however, Scripture is not nonplussed (13:18b); as the psalmist laments, 'he who ate my bread, has lifted his heel against me' (Psa. 41:9, ESV).

Table fellowship, the entertaining of guests and eating with them, was, and still is, a supreme sign of acceptance in Middle Eastern culture. To abuse such kindness by betraying it is the most obnoxious infringement of the first law of hospitality, what Gordon Wakefield calls 'the nadir of deception and enmity'.[16]

In giving advance warning of just such a betrayal, Jesus will only confirm His identification with the One Creator God who had revealed Himself to Moses and Isaiah as the transcendent and self-sufficient 'I am' (13:19b).

But this makes acceptance or rejection of Him a matter of absolute and eternal significance (13:20). The seriousness of the situation is underscored by His repeated 'Truly, truly …' (ESV). Nothing is more certain than that everything hangs on our reception of the One who occupies a position of 'unshared nearness' to the Father and, subsequently, of those whom He in turn commissions as His authorised agents!

The imminence of such treachery and the terrible consequences that will flow from it for all concerned weigh heavily upon Him. It disturbs Him deeply (*'tarasso'* again as in 12:27): '… Jesus was troubled in spirit …' (13:21).

If Jesus shows serenity throughout the narrative, it is born of His trust in the Father's sovereignty and nourished by the Father's love. It is not unruffled peace. In conventional terms, says Archbishop Rowan Williams, Jesus was a 'singularly unpeaceful person'.

At every turn His poise is hard won and grounded in a settled sense of purpose which is not derived from living in idyllic surroundings far removed from the tension of human existence.

He has often been exasperated by His disciples' slowness to understand; now one of them is about to betray Him. From this His spirit recoils in horror.

It is as if the breach of hospitality will open up a wound in the divine fellowship to reveal the victorious vulnerability of God's love.

13:22

Jesus' warning about treachery in the camp causes consternation among the other disciples. The mood, already tense, tightens with uncertainty: 'Is it me, Lord?'

Sad as it is, some go out from the fellowship of Christ who by their departure – and sometimes by the manner of their leaving – prove that they never really belonged to us (cf. 1 John 2:19).

Judas may have to go.

Sadly, too, many of us remain oblivious and lacking in discernment of the danger that dines at our table.

Judas will have to go!

Sadder still, the infusion of evil pollutes the atmosphere of trust. Anxious and crippling self-analysis breaks out: 'Is it me, Lord?' Judas' legacy is the gift of suspicion which, in turn, breeds fear, self-doubt and uncertainty in the community.

Judas must go.

13:26–30

And Judas will go.

Jesus dismisses him to do his deadly work. But not before Jesus makes love's last appeal. 'On the night in which He was betrayed', He offers the sop to the traitor.

Judas resists even this final token of friendship. He turns his back on the circle of light and walks out into the enveloping darkness.

Judas does go!

'And it was night' – is all John needs to add (13:30).

13:31–38

With Judas gone, events can move swiftly to their climax.

But in John's unique and paradoxical angle of vision, the coming glory is conflated with the crucifixion.

The very showdown which the departure of Judas sets in motion will prove to be the showcase of God's glory.

The deeper the darkness, the brighter the light will shine.

The Son of Man will achieve the glory marked out for Him in Daniel's strange vision by treading the even stranger path of suffering. The sequence of cross, resurrection, ascension, is fused by John into one extended exaltation.

The mutual glorification of Father and Son is not self-serving, since each is devoted to the other's best interests. God is revealed to be not a solitary monad consumed by self-regard or cramped by self-absorption. Rather, what we are seeing unveiled before our eyes is the glory of divine love which is for ever being outpoured and received within the Trinity.

So as we watch the worst that evil can do, we see the best that God can do. Just where God – Father and Son – appear to be most dishonoured and disgraced, is where God is most gloriously revealed as self-giving love.

Jesus points to the paradox by talking of doing a vanishing act! At this point the disciples – they are piqued to learn – are in no better a position than their opponents for, like them, they cannot go where He is going (13:33)!

As Kelly and Moloney point out, 'Neither party can understand the Fatherward direction of his path.'[17]

13:34–35

The new commandment Jesus gives is not without parallel in the Old Testament and elsewhere. But the commandment is 'new' not because it has never been *heard* before, but because it has never been *seen* before!

It is measured by a new standard – 'as I have loved you'. It will take its rise from the unprecedented self-giving love of His cross. What is called for here is love in action, love that stoops to meet the lowliest needs of others.

As such it takes us to the heart of the 'new' covenant heralded at the Last Supper and inaugurated by His blood shed in sacrificial death.

Love is a currency much devalued in the modern world. We confuse it so often with a passing mood or a fleeting attraction that we wonder how love could possibly be commanded!

Some Christians are so concerned to overcome this problem that they seem to want to eliminate all feelings from Christian loving. In much discussion, this is usually styled, somewhat pompously, 'agape-love', under the misapprehension that the Greek word *agape* is special and somehow in itself defines a certain quality of love. This is linguistically untenable as Don Carson has no difficulty in showing. But on this spurious authority, some writers reduce Christian love to a cold, rather mechanical and dispassionate, altruism.[18]

Love is certainly action on behalf of others. But, according to 1 Corinthians 13:1, what seems pure altruism can in fact mask an absence of genuine love!

No, a safer guide than word-games is Jesus and His '… as I have loved you'. And who can imagine that His utter self-giving on the cross was passionless or lacking in fervent feelings towards us! And it is precisely this whole-hearted, full-blooded, practical love that is commanded by Jesus and made possible by His cross and the gift of the Spirit.

And such love is commanded!

Some scholars suggest that the Farewell Discourses in John are the New Testament equivalent of the book of Deuteronomy where Moses bids farewell to the generation on the verge of entering the promised land. Certainly the same themes occur of knowing God and loving God and keeping His commandments.

If these Deuteronomic echoes can be heard in these marvellous discourses, then we learn something significant about Jesus. Not only is He putting Himself in the place of Moses as the mediator of God's covenant blessings and responsibilities, He is putting Himself in the place of God by issuing further and new commandments to the people of God.

He issues here the 'eleventh commandment'!

This tough love will be the distinguishing mark of the new people of God. And we may ourselves be surprised by the large space created in our hearts by the hospitality of the cross.

Carson comments,

> If Christian love for other Christians were nothing more than the shared affection of mutually compatible people, it would be indistinguishable from pagan love for pagans or from tax collectors' love for tax collectors. The reason why Christian love will stand and bear witness to Jesus is that it is a display, for Jesus' sake, of mutual love among social incompatibles.[19]

Karl Barth was asked once: 'Will we one day see our loved ones again in heaven?' He replied: 'Not only the loved ones!'

If we honoured Jesus' legacy by loving as He loves us, the world might know we were His disciples.

13:36–38

In a high-octane mixture of bravado and desperation, Peter

clamours to know where exactly Jesus is going so as to follow Him there. Afterwards, he is told, then you may go there!

Peter then characteristically boasts of his readiness to outdo the others by laying down his life for Jesus (v.37).

You can sense the sad tenderness of Jesus in His wistful reply: 'You will, will you …?'

And one day he will, but only long after his prideful self-confidence is laid in the dust.

As Don Carson sardonically observes, 'Sadly, good intentions in a secure room after good food are far less attractive in a darkened garden with a hostile mob.'[20]

In one of his last books, Lewis Smedes ponders whether he would be willing to die for Jesus if it would guarantee the world's restoration. He thinks he might, but can't be sure. In any case, he ruefully reflects, as far as we are concerned, dying for the world is not the hard part. 'The hard part comes,' he says, 'when He tells me to show my passion for a world that works right by living the sort of life that makes people say: "Ah, so that is how people are going to live when righteousness takes over the world." This, not dying for the world, is the hard part.'[21]

Again 'afterwards' will answer all questions.

Meanwhile, the disciples cannot fathom nor can they follow where He is going. He will 'tread the winepress alone …' and 'none of the ransomed' will ever know 'how deep were the waters crossed …'

Much has to happen which only He can endure.

Many things have to be taught them which only He can say.

His going to the Father will leave a vacuum for the Holy

Spirit to fill.

His departure will create a space for a loving community to occupy.

The hospitality of the cross will in truth evoke the hospitality of the heart.

NB

13:31–38 sets a structure for the rest of the Discourse.

13:31–32	glorification	glorification	**17:1–26**
13:33	departure	departure	**16:4–33**
13:34–35	love/world's hatred	love/world's hate	**15:1–16:3**
13:36–38	journey/going?	journey/going?	**14:1–31**

Questions:

Peter's:	13:36–38
Thomas's:	14:5–7
Philip's:	14:8–21
Judas's (not Iscariot)	14:22–31

CHAPTER THREE

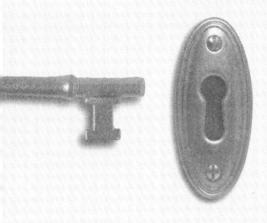

THE JOURNEY TO THE FATHER'S HOUSE

(John 14)

The Legacy of Jesus

His promise
His Spirit
His peace

JOHN 14

[1]'Do not let your hearts be troubled. Trust in God; trust also in me. [2]In my Father's house are many rooms; if it were not so, I would have told you. I am going there to prepare a place for you. [3]And if I go and prepare a place for you, I will come back and take you to be with me that you also may be where I am. [4]You know the way to the place where I am going.'

[5]Thomas said to him, 'Lord, we don't know where you are going, so how can we know the way?'

[6]Jesus answered, 'I am the way and the truth and the life. No-one comes to the Father except through me. [7]If you really knew me, you would know my Father as well. From now on, you do know him and have seen him.'

[8]Philip said, 'Lord, show us the Father and that will be enough for us.'

[9]Jesus answered: 'Don't you know me, Philip, even after I have been among you such a long time? Anyone who has seen me has seen the Father. How can you say, "Show us the Father"? [10]Don't you believe that I am in the Father, and that the Father is in me? The words I say to you are not just my own. Rather, it is the Father, living in me, who is doing his work. [11]Believe me when I say that I am in the Father and the Father is in me; or at least believe on the evidence of the miracles themselves. [12]I tell you the truth, anyone who has faith in me will do what I have been doing. He will do even greater things than these, because I am going to the Father.

[13]And I will do whatever you ask in my name, so that the Son may bring glory to the Father. [14]You may ask me for anything in my name, and I will do it.

[15]'If you love me, you will obey what I command. [16]And I will ask the Father, and he will give you another Counsellor to be with you for ever – [17]the Spirit of truth. The world cannot accept him, because it neither sees him nor knows him. But you know him, for he lives with you and will be in you. [18]I will not leave you as orphans; I will come to you. [19]Before long, the world will not see me any more, but you will see me. Because I live, you also will live. [20]On that day you will realise that I am in my Father, and you are in me, and I am in you. [21]Whoever has my commands and obeys them, he is the one who loves me. He who loves me will be loved by my Father, and I too will love him and show myself to him.'

[22]Then Judas (not Judas Iscariot) said, 'But, Lord, why do you intend to show yourself to us and not to the world?'

[23]Jesus replied, 'If anyone loves me, he will obey my teaching. My Father will love him, and we will come to him and make our home with him. [24]He who does not love me will not obey my teaching. These words you hear are not my own; they belong to the Father who sent me.

[25]'All this I have spoken while still with you. [26]But the Counsellor, the Holy Spirit, whom the Father will send in my name, will teach you all things and will remind you of everything I have said to you. [27]Peace I leave with you; my

peace I give you. I do not give to you as the world gives. Do not let your hearts be troubled and do not be afraid.

[28]'You heard me say, "I am going away and I am coming back to you." If you loved me, you would be glad that I am going to the Father, for the Father is greater than I. [29]I have told you now before it happens, so that when it does happen you will believe. [30]I will not speak with you much longer, for the prince of this world is coming. He has no hold on me, [31]but the world must learn that I love the Father and that I do exactly what my Father has commanded me.

'Come now; let us leave.'

14:1–3

In these memorable words of Jesus, talk of leaving and returning, of the journey and the way, merges with metaphors of homecoming to engender further images of hospitality and mutual indwelling. But the disciples are in no mood for sorting out mixed metaphors however comforting. They are deafened to good news by the dread word of His departure. The trumpets may be sounding on the other side but they can hear only the last post, as the flag is lowered on the kingdom of God.

So the disciples are troubled.

And why wouldn't they be?

'You're leaving, Lord?'
It would have scared me witless, the thought of Him leaving!
Bewilderment and distress engulf them.

'If Peter falls, where does that leave any of us?'
Peter's predicted denial coming as it does on the back of Judas'
sudden and suspicious exit, must have left the disciples reeling,
their confidence melting away; if Peter the Rock crumbles, who
can stand?

'You expect us to do the job without you, Lord?'
Each of us wants to say, 'I will follow you, Lord' but then we look
at His ministry and death and say: 'Follow that!'

The enormity of their task ahead may finally be dawning on
the disciples and they don't feel up to it!

'You're not making sense, Lord'
Jesus is usually so plain speaking; now He seems to be speaking
in riddles (cf. 16:25). Peter had started this discussion by asking
where Jesus was going (13:36). Perhaps he was regretting it.

In a crisis like this, the chest tightens in the icy grip of fear, the
heart races, the mind defaults to the unthinkable.

Trouble puts an almost unbearable strain on trust.

In the shadow of the cross, we might have expected the disciples
to give Jesus emotional and spiritual support; instead He offers
it to them.

In His legacy, He leaves us an astonishing promise.
He consoles them: to be sure, His 'going' involves going to the
cross, but it also involves 'going to the Father' to 'prepare a place'
for His people.

It is worth noting what this does *not mean*. Jesus is not saying that He is going to heaven and that then, when He gets there, He will prepare for us.

Rather, He means that by the entire movement of His going to the Father – in death, resurrection and ascension – He prepares a place for us. 'Many mansions' is the AV's seventeenth-century attempt at translating a word – *monai* – which was an expression for modest dwelling places. Thus, as Gary Burge says, this promise 'should not build a picture for us of heavenly palatial residences'.[1]

Christ's words, 'I will come back' might conceivably refer to His resurrection, as they seem to do elsewhere in these Farewell Discourses, or to His coming back in the presence of the Holy Spirit (ie first at 14:18 where He surely refers to His resurrection appearances; and 14:23 where the coming to make a home with us surely refers to the indwelling work of the Spirit).

Both of these are true, but since both are foretastes of our future fellowship with Him, it seems best to read His words here as a *firm promise of His second coming.*

There is something elusive about Jesus' words and we might have wished He had said more. As always we are on the edge of mystery here. But troubled hearts have never failed to take comfort from this priceless promise.

Whatever shape the redeemed future takes, Jesus assures us that it is an expansive place, which is being carefully and lovingly prepared with ample room in it for all God's faithful people! Above all, He promises that we will be wherever He is, and that surely will be heaven on earth for us all.

Of this splendid prospect, His appearances after death, risen and alive, are all the guarantee we need. And we sense that, however indescribable, the future will be like going home.

The disciples desperately need the strange comfort that Jesus is offering their troubled hearts. What causes Him His unique turmoil (12:27; 13:21) threatens to overwhelm them. The disciples are staring bleakly into the black hole of abandonment. They can feel their hopes and dreams disappearing into it.

I empathise with them. I have known Jesus as my friend since I was seven years old. Even if I now live for long stretches without a sense of His personal presence, the thought of His absence terrifies me; how much more for them who had walked and talked with Him in the flesh.

No Christian can stay sane and faithful without at least once in a while staring into that abyss and wondering if it's all too good to be true.

Such thoughts are enough to trouble any heart; especially any heart that has for a moment entertained the hope that everything might be different. If we dare to believe in God at all, we will have to stake all on Jesus.

Again, when it comes to talk of heaven or the better world coming, some of us have a more vivid anticipation of it than others. For my part, I peer towards it as though through a thick mist. But where my head aches, my heart aches more. With C.S. Lewis, my troubled heart snatches at the scent of a flower we have not yet seen, the breathe of breeze in an airtight room, the echo of a song we have not yet sung.

Perhaps it is true that my lingering discontent is, after all, a deep, unspeakable, longing for heaven.

In the end, like a drowning man, I cling to His assurance: '*If it were not so, I would have told you …*'

This troubled heart trusts you, Lord Jesus.

As Lewis Smedes says, 'when hope is based on a promise, hope and trust become one and the same thing.'[2]

14:4–11

Thomas and Philip now take up the questioning.

Thomas takes up Peter's earlier question: 'Where are you going?' (v.5a; cf. 13:36). He adds to it a further matter that is confusing them: 'how can we know the way?' (v.5b).

In other words – as Craig Koester helpfully summarises – there are two issues on which they are pressing for clarification:

- *the destination (where are You going?)* and
- *the journey (how can we know the way?)*

(a) as to His *destination*, He makes it clear:

- He is going to God as He has come from God (13:1,3).
- He is going to the Father (14:12, 28; 17:11), to the One who sent Him (16:5).
- He is going home to the Father's house and glory, there to prepare a place for us (14:1–3).

So the answer to the question, 'Where are You going?' is: *He is going to the Father to share His glory again.*

(b) as to the *journey* He will make:

His way of glorifying the Father will be by walking the way of suffering, and death on the cross. In the defining sense in which this is about to happen to Him, no one else can go this way (13:33).

Afterwards, derivatively and in a secondary sense, others will walk this way too (13:36).

So the answer to the question, 'What is the way He is going?' is: *He is going the way of the cross.*

The discussion is brought to a head by one of Jesus' great self-defining statements: 'I am the way and the truth and the life' (v.6).

HE IS THE WAY

His unique going to the Father is the only way we come to God.

His cruciform way of going is the journey we must embark on if we are to follow in His steps.

So Jesus is the Way for us in both senses:

(a) He is the only way for us to come to God (v.6b)

The only way we can reach God, come to the Father, reconnect with the Source of our life and destiny is through Jesus. He does not merely show us how to get there but is Himself the way to get there!

Jesus does not merely open up the way as a trailblazer might but, as Kelly and Moloney rightly stress, 'He is from beginning to end the way to the Father.'[3]

Now, as we realise in our day, if He had said: 'I am *a* way and *a* truth and *a* life' no one would have taken exception; in fact no one would have taken any notice! In our culture which celebrates relativism and pluralism in which all roads to God are valid, and truth is what seems true for you, this statement of Jesus sounds impossibly exclusive and intolerant!

But given the Old Testament revelation of the One Creator God over against all other so-called gods, there can be no doubt that the One who is presented to us in the gospel as the Incarnation of that God, as His unique logos or self-expression, will carry with Him the same exclusive reality and challenge.[4]

David Ball draws out the significance of the link being made between the prophetic view of God and John's view of Jesus. 'If … the "I am" sayings of John's Gospel deliberately allude to the similar sayings in Isaiah, it is highly significant that Jesus is not only identified with Yahweh, but he is identified with a phrase which excludes all other rivals from the worship of the LORD.'[5]

But it is precisely the exclusive nature of this message that makes it so *inclusive*.

Why would the One Creator God leave His world to its own devices in finding a Saviour, groping around in confusion among a million different options and opinions? It is surely an act of great mercy to penetrate the darkness of doubt and uncertainty and to put the spotlight on the one way needed to find salvation.

I agree with Craig Koester when he says, 'The absolute quality of the statement "I am the Way", expresses the absolute quality of God's love for the world.'[6]

So the first apostles were unabashed as they went out with good news for a multi-cultural Greco–Roman world, riddled with alternative gods, cults and sects. They had every incentive

– not least being spared martyrdom – for toning down this uncompromising message and settling for a niche for Jesus in the pantheon of the gods. But they did not.

From the monotheistic atmosphere of a hostile Jerusalem to the sceptical pagan polytheistic culture of Athens, they boldly proclaimed that there is salvation in no one else, for there is 'no other name under heaven given to men by which we must be saved' and the world's standards and values measured and judged (Acts 4:12; 17:31).

Not long before his death, Lesslie Newbigin was asked by a journalist why he accepted the teaching of Jesus as true rather than that of other great teachers of religion. Newbigin replied, 'because Jesus was raised from the dead and they weren't'! It would be in 'that day' – the day that matches 'His hour', the day beyond resurrection, Jesus told them – that they would realise who had really been and really was (14:20).

Philip now enters the dialogue, as he presses for further reassurance by asking: 'Lord, show us the Father …' (14:8).

The issue all along has been the *truth* about God and His relationship with Jesus.

This is crystalised in the 'I am …' statements.

Once again there are strong echoes of Isaiah. In Isaiah's trial scenario the issue before the court of nations is: who is the true God. 'I am,' says Yahweh; 'I am the first and the last, I am he' (Isa. 41:4; 43:14; 48:12).

Beyond Isaiah, of course, lies the foundational revelation God made to Moses that 'I AM WHO I AM' and that 'I AM' has sent him (Exod. 3:14).

Later in the Exodus narrative, Moses desires to see God, asking: 'show me your glory' (33:18). Moses, we know, was offered only the back view of God through a cleft in the rock.

When Philip asks: 'Lord, show us the Father ...' Jesus replies: 'Whoever has seen me has seen the Father ...' (v.9, ESV). Philip and the others are invited – as Paul later was on the Damascus road – to see the glory of God in the face of Jesus Christ.

The apostolic testimony to Jesus' aliveness can communicate with us by being translated into the faith terminology of *knowing, seeing* and *believing*, as John notes in vv.7, 9–10.

To come home to the Father through Jesus is to:

- *know (v.7) and understand that Jesus embodies God and therefore to understand and know Him is to know God*
- *see (v.9) and recognise who Jesus really is as the Incarnate God and so to see and recognise the Father*
- or put another way – it is to *believe (v.10) that the Father and Son mutually indwell each other and so to believe in Him is to believe in God.*

All sections of the Church need to go deeper with the unequivocal statement of Jesus that He is the Way (14:6).

Liberals need to hear its uncompromising and biblically authorised exclusivism; to forgo the fear of offending and of treading on politically correct toes; and to resist being drawn into a New Age type of spirituality in which true Godness is melted down into some impersonal, warm soup of transcendent feelings.

Evangelicals need to take much more seriously than we have ever done the implications of Him saying: 'Anyone who has seen me has seen the Father': namely, that Jesus is the final word, the ultimate expression and demonstration of what God is like.

The exclusive message we proclaim stems from a God who comes to self-expression in stooping to wash the dirty feet of ordinary people and that such self-giving love defines the shape this God takes in our world.

(b) He is the only way for us to live for God

This is strong implication, brought to the surface in the Fourth Gospel all around this text and encapsulated in 14:15.

To love Him is to obey His commandments which involve living as He lived, freely obedient to the gracious will of His Father, and loving as He loved with the Father's self-giving love.

I Did it My Way was a ballad made famous by Frank Sinatra. It is one of the top ten songs now chosen to be sung at weddings. It sums up the self-serving life. 'I Did it My Way' suggested Os Guinness, 'is the song they sing in hell! Jesus did it God's way and His is the song they sing in heaven!'

To follow Him as the Way is to follow in His way.

To follow Him as the Way is to know and understand Him in His unique relationship to God as the unique Son sent by the Father; it is to believe that Father and Son share a divine life.

To confess Him as the Way is to call Him the crucified and risen One.

To follow Him who is the Way is to embrace the path of discipleship and – if need be – to be willing to walk the path of suffering and self-giving as the path of glory, as He did.

So in the Acts of the Apostles, Luke tells us that the first designation which attached to Christians was 'followers of the Way'.

To follow the Way is to walk in His way.

He is the Way: no one comes to the Father except by Him.

He is the Way: no one comes except by coming His way.

In 14:10–11 Jesus reaffirms the unique unity of will and action, thought and word, that exists between Him and His Father. But this unity is not merely that which might exist between master and servant where the servant intuitively double-guesses the master's intentions. Jesus goes much further than this in explaining the harmony between Him and God as a mysterious mutual indwelling.

Gary Burge astutely comments, 'Jesus is therefore not making a claim simply to possess some functional equivalence with the Father, saying in effect that he is doing what the Father does ... It is not simply that Jesus is sent on a divine mission on behalf of the Father, but that the Father himself is on a divine mission in the life of his Son'.[7]

Which is why the Father is glorified not just *by* the Son but *in* the Son (v.13b). The Son's words and works are the joint witness to the reality of His unique union with the Father and to His revelation of the truth about the one true God.

As is well known, the miracles and wonders recorded in the Synoptic Gospels, become, in the Fourth Gospel, 'signs' ('*semeia*') which signify the presence of the Father's saving rule and are intended to lead us to faith (John 20:30–31). In John's narrative, signs are interwoven with the 'I am' statements so that each illuminates the other. If you can't hear the words, accept the evidence of the works (14:11).

George Hunsberger summarises well: 'If his own presence was a *sign* of the reign of God, and his deeds were *signposts* pointing to it, his verbal proclamation of the meaning of his presence and deeds, added his *signature*'.[8]

14:12 '... GREATER WORKS ...'?

These can scarcely be more spectacular than those Jesus did, notably the raising of Lazarus from the dead!

Nor, I think, does this mean simply that there will be more of them in a quantitative sense since such works will no longer be confined by His Incarnation. Rather, the works the disciples will do will be 'greater' because, after His death, resurrection and ascension, they will be works done in a greater realm of reality.

They will be greater, in other words, because He goes to the Father.

A somewhat similar statement occurs in Matthew 11:11: 'I tell you the truth: Among those born of women there has not risen anyone greater than John the Baptist; yet he who is least in the kingdom of heaven is *greater* than he' (my italics).

The least disciple is greater than the mighty John not because he or she is more worthy or more devout but because he or she lives in a realm that John could only prepare for – the realm of God's kingdom as introduced by Jesus. (Matthew 11:12 makes this clear.)

With Jesus' exaltation and the gift of the Spirit, a new era opens up, with powerful new possibilities. So the 'greater things' are the things Jesus will achieve in and through His believing disciples, from His 'greater' place of authority and lordship, by the impartation of the Spirit.

14:13 GUARANTEED PRAYING?

Only by faith in Him as the ascended and glorified One who has indeed gone to the Father, will these 'greater works' be done. And one vital way in which this faith in Him is exercised is in prayer.

With His going to the Father, prayer too moves into a new era, becoming prayer *in His name*.

What does this mean?

Well, it surely does not mean that we merely tack the name 'Jesus' onto the end of our prayers in some formulaic way. When some who did not have a relationship with Jesus tried this in the early days of the Church, it did not work and proved dangerously self-defeating (Acts 19:13–16)!

Nor does it mean that we decide what we want to do or want done and then we ask Jesus to endorse it by signing His name to it! Rather, prayer 'in His name' is prayer authorised by Jesus. It is prayer compatible with the revelation He has brought.

It is not so much about asking for Him to back the work we are doing, as about making ourselves available for Him to continue to work in us, among us and through us.

We pray 'in His name' so that all our asking, wishing, planning and doing, may be shaped and sanctioned by His authority. We pray 'in His name' so that all our ambitions and activity may honour His name, exemplify what He stands for, confirm His lordship and align with His great interest which is to see the Father glorified.

It is in this way that prayer plays a vital role in the new order of things and further facilitates His achieving of 'greater works' in and through us.

Gary Burge summarises well: 'Such answered prayer is another "great work" that Jesus will accomplish among them. The disciples' lives will be a continuation of Jesus' life in the world. Both great deeds and answered prayer glorify the Father because it is Jesus who is at work still accomplishing them.'[9]

Is this not another example of the amazing humility of Jesus? That He should be willing for the deeds done by Him in His own flesh to be – as it were – upstaged by the deeds done by Him in their flesh.

In Kelly and Moloney's words,

> he subverts the whole self-assertive structure of the glory of this world by allowing for the disciples' 'greater works' … The realm of glory and true life means not only the Son's self-surrender to the Father, but also his self-effacement in the 'greater works' to be performed by his followers in the time of another paraclete. [10]

14:15–17 THE LEGACY OF JESUS: HE LEFT US HIS SPIRIT

In all the legacy of Jesus to us, nothing is greater than that of the bestowal of the Holy Spirit.

The Holy Spirit is the *crowning gift* (cf. John 7:39). He is the object of the Son's ultimate request ('I will ask the Father …').

He comes as the consummate outflow of the Father's self-giving ('… and he will give you …' cf. Acts 2:36–38).

And this gift of God in the Holy Spirit is irrevocable, never to be withdrawn, a perennial and refreshing presence ('… to be with you for ever …').

What we are promised here, it needs to be emphasised, is the *personal character of the Holy Spirit*. This is underscored by the fact that even though the word '*pneuma*' is neuter, the masculine pronoun is used – 'he'.

It is surely worth re-emphasising in our day, that the Holy Spirit should never be thought of as an 'it' but as a 'Person', not merely a force to be reckoned with but a presence to be respected and enjoyed.

I think of an occasion only a week or so before writing these sentences when the personality of the Holy Spirit came home to me in a powerful way. I was driving south to see a friend on a clear and calm day and listening to a tape of Gordon Fee lecturing on Pauline theology at Regent College, Vancouver. He spoke compellingly of the personal nature of the Holy Spirit and of how our sin can grieve Him (Eph. 4:30). I was suddenly swamped with surges of grief for the way in which – in a particular season of my life many years ago – I had hurt the Holy Spirit, and I wept copiously, hopefully with real regret and deep repentance for the pain I had caused Him.

As Fee notes, 'One can only grieve a person, and our misdeeds grieve God, who has come to indwell us individually and corporately by his Spirit.'[11]

The impersonal terms often used to describe the *work* of the Spirit in Scripture – fire, wind, oil – should not mislead us into depersonalising *Him*, or make us wary that His operations will depersonalise *us*.

Tom Smail writes,

> The combination of otherness and self-giving defines the relationship of persons to each other, and just that combination marks the relationship of the Spirit to us. We, as humans, receive the divine Spirit; but, he does not become human and we do not become divine. He gives himself to us and remains himself; we receive him and remain who we are.[12]

In this respect, it is not untrue to speak of the *Christlikeness of the Spirit*. In being described as 'another paraclete' there is no doubt that, in some sense, '*another*' implies '*like Jesus*'. As Jesus has been 'with them' for three years, the Spirit will be 'with them' for ever.

In several important respects, their activities are parallel, so that what is said about Jesus is said about the Spirit.

- Like Jesus, the Spirit is given and sent by the Father (14:16,26/3:16, and *passim*), is not received by the world (14:17/1:11; 5:43; 12:48), teaches (14:26/7:14ff.; 8:20) and bears witness (15:26/5:31ff.; 8:13f.; 18:37 etc).
- Like Jesus, the Spirit does not speak of Himself, only what He has heard (16:13/7:17; 8:26–28,38; 12:49ff.)
- Like Jesus, He represents truth; as the 'Spirit of Truth' (14:17;

16:13) He brings to remembrance (14:26f.) all that had been said by the One who is the Truth (14:6; 18:37).

Not surprisingly, elsewhere in the New Testament, He is described as the 'Spirit of Christ' or the 'Spirit of Jesus'. So, humbly, the Spirit subsumes Himself under the role of glorifying Jesus (16:15).

Since the Incarnation, we might say, the one creative Holy Spirit of God never comes to us except freighted with the character and qualities of Jesus.

Post-Pentecost, in Jim Packer's words, 'The Spirit makes known the personal presence in and with the Christian and the church of the risen, reigning Saviour, the Jesus of history, who is the Christ of faith.'[13]

Jesus describes the Spirit as the 'paraklete' ('parakletos').

The word literally refers to someone who is 'called alongside' with a view to helping someone else, though 'helper' (ESV) seems weak.

Comforter is misleading, except in the old English sense of 'giving strength to'. A cameo in the Bayeux tapestry shows King Harry 'comforting' his troops, by prodding them into action with his lance!

Counsellor is better, but concedes too much to a therapeutic culture which reduces everything to psychological terms.

Exhorter and encourager are useful since *paraklesis* is the term used in the New Testament for exhortation. But this still misses an important connection with the trial motif which is central to John's Gospel.

In fact, *parakletos* almost certainly retains the forensic connotation it had in wider usage, and is best translated as '*advocate*' in a legal sense. This meaning fits well the overall picture John paints in his Gospel, of Jesus – and the disciples – on trial for the truth before a hostile world.

Andrew Lincoln offers a helpful summary,

> Both his earlier witness in the public ministry and his later witness before Pilate are that of a Paraclete, advocating his own case, which is also the case of God, in the trial of truth with the world. Conversely, the Spirit is continuing this forensic role of Jesus in the continuing lawsuit after the glorification of Jesus.[14]

The Holy Spirit is another 'advocate' like Jesus. He will stand by the disciples just as Jesus has done. Just as Jesus has comforted, helped, encouraged and exhorted them, so the Spirit will act as 'another *counsel for the defence* in the great contest with the world over the truth of God'.[15]

As such He offers no comfort or counsel to mere armchair Christians. But wherever and however you are 'on trial' today for your faith and witness, the Holy Spirit is with you to defend and prompt and support you.

In the legal contest over truth, the Spirit is *the Spirit of Truth* who represents the truth of God embodied in Jesus.

Truth carries Old Testament connotations of 'faithfulness and integrity'; its Greek connotations set it over against falsehood, error and unreality. So truth is *reliable reality*, that reliable reality which God is, and which is made known in Jesus.

Truth is the reality of *this* God, the Father, incarnate in *this* Person, Jesus, the Son, for *this* purpose, to save, as it comes to full expression in *this* kind of death with *this* particular sequel, resurrection.

So we must perhaps speak of the *otherness of the Spirit* whom 'the world cannot accept ... because it neither sees him nor knows him ...'

This is meant not in the obvious sense that the world is often so materialistic that it is blind to the realm of Spirit. In fact, as William Temple once said, Christianity is the most materialistic of religions, since it is founded on creation and refounded on incarnation. Now as then, the world is surely awash with 'spiritualities'. All the more necessary then, to define *our* spirituality by reference to the Holy Spirit of God as SPIRITuality', as Gordon Fee contends.

In fact, Jesus says, the world is no more willing to acknowledge the one true Spirit than it is to recognise and accept Him!

So the gift of the Holy Spirit to us inevitably sets up a counter-cultural tension between us and the world.

But what does 'world' or 'kosmos' denote in John's Gospel?

- 'kosmos' has its obvious meaning of 'the created world', and is used in this sense in John's cosmic vision (1:10a,b)
- 'kosmos' is used more particularly of the *world of humanity*, which is the sense, in all probability, of 3:16: 'God so loved the world ...'
- 'but 'kosmos' is most often used by John in *a negative or*

pejorative, moral sense (1:10c '... the world did not recognise him').

In other words, more often than not, usually plain from the context, what John means by 'the world' is the world as organised in rebellion against God.

In this view, there is an emphasis on the structured reality of resistance to God's will and ways, which is more than the sum of individual rebellion and sin.

Walter Wink, in his profound contemporary trilogy on the powers, speaks of the 'human sociological realm as it exists in estrangement from God'.[16]

Very helpfully, Wink suggests that we might highlight this negative and sociological analysis by translating the word 'world' or 'kosmos' as '*the domination system*'.

According to John 18:36, Jesus Himself professed that His kingdom while 'in this world' was not 'of this world'. As Wink puts it, 'the new reality ... does not take its rise from the domination system'.

The domination system dictates what we *believe*, by offering, in Wink's words, 'the acceptable beliefs that society at any given time declares to be credible ...'[17]

No wonder that in pre-democratic South Africa, when the police came to the door to enforce apartheid laws, people said: 'The "system's" here' or 'the "system" says ...'

The 'system' teaches us what to *value* in terms of success, money, violence, militarism, fashion and so on. In fact it wants to dictate how we *see* the world, and it employs sophisticated media technology to shape our perceptions of reality. It is in this sense, to use Paul's phrase, that the God of this world has blinded the minds of unbelievers.

At this point, we need to be careful not to allow the negative connotation of the term 'world' to shut us off completely from its more positive sense. Christians are not against God's created order, as if they prefer a rarified, ethereal spirituality. In fact, we celebrate the materiality of the world God made, relish its beauty and seek, despite the Fall, to preserve its goodness. We resist any gnostic attempt to downgrade the physicality of the body, and by doing so, undermine the incarnational foundations of our faith.

Nor should we misconstrue Jesus when He says that His kingdom is 'not of this world' as if it deals only in spiritual realities that are unconnected with the world of politics, economics, sexuality and family. But where it is appropriate – which is often – replace 'world' by 'domination system' and the lights go on! '… the domination system hates you …' '… but take heart, I have overcome the domination system …'

So, as we explore what Jesus says about the Spirit here and in chapters 15 and 16, it becomes obvious that the Spirit is a strongly *counter-cultural* force in our lives. He will, as we say, comfort the disturbed but disturb the comfortable.

The Spirit will always be a *subversive presence*, undermining all oppressive and dehumanising structures in society. The Spirit will at the very least, embolden us to question the cultural norms and accepted wisdom of our world. The Spirit will give us courage to bear witness to the truth that sets the oppressed free. The Spirit will not simply bring us comfort and peace and joy in a way that insulates us from the way things are out there. The Spirit will lead us to revalue what has been dishonoured – from marriage to the status of the unborn – to look with new eyes on the complacent way we connive at unjust practices in society, and to go against the grain in believing the revealed truth about God and confessing that Jesus is the only way to salvation.

To return to our text (14:17), it is in the 'system's' interests to prevent us seeing or recognising the reality of the Holy Spirit lest we see and recognise the reality of the lordship of Jesus and of His Father.

A world built on lies, deceit and unreality is a stranger to the Spirit of truth. But the Spirit comes alongside you to enable you speak and live the truth, helping you to follow Jesus who is the truth.

Jesus promises that the Spirit when He comes will live '*in*' His disciples. As to what this extraordinary *indwelling* entails, let's listen to the spiritual masters.

In this way, says Austin Farrer, just as He did with Jesus,

> he becomes the Spirit of those he indwells, and molds himself upon the form of their life … No one supposes that, when the Spirit indwells us, he takes up a local habitation in some corner of us, like a lodger in a house. No, what is meant is that his action becomes the soul of our action, his mind the soul of our thought; he shapes himself to us so that he may shape us to himself. A human act is performed, a human life is lived, a human aspiration aroused, and yet all

this is the very act, and life, and love of God in us.[18]

And here is Samuel Chadwick.

> The indwelling is that of a real, personal, spiritual Presence. It is not a gift that can be located somewhere in the brain or heart of a man, but a personal Spirit that indwells another personality; a personality within a personality by which the Spirit becomes the life of my life, the soul of my soul; an indwelling that secures identity without confusion, and possession without absorption.[19]

14:18

'I will not leave you as orphans; I will come to you.'

If the earlier promise of Jesus' 'coming back' referred to His second coming, this 'I will come to you' almost certainly speaks of His return to His disciples after the Resurrection. The context supports this. Though He goes away (in death), the disciples will see Him (v.20).

What stunning promises these were to them and what a reassurance for us. '… you will see … you will live … you will know…' (14:19–20).

Jesus will go through death and out the other side.

He will not simply be a resuscitated corpse, returning to His old mode of existence. Rather, He will enter into a new phase of existence, characterised by resurrection life and in the reality of that new creation life, meet them again!

Many people, growing weary and cynical in our modern world,

no longer ask 'Is there life after death?' but 'Is there life before death?' But Jesus steps out from the other side of death to meet both conditions. He alone gives hope and substance to what lies beyond death in God's kingdom future. And He alone gives joy and meaning to the life to be lived before death in God's kingdom present.

Whether now or then, in the perplexing present or uncertain future, He will not leave us orphans. He will gather us to His Father and fold us in the loving embrace of His Father's family.

In the meantime of the historical process, the challenge remains. For His words are not just any words, uttered among a myriad others, but they are the words of the Word, the speech of Him who is the final utterance, the Father's own ultimate self-expression.

Evangelical Christians like me, Pauline converts as it were, are often embarrassed by the plain commands of Jesus. Not wanting to take them in wooden literalness, we seldom take them seriously. The American humorist, Garrison Keillor, discomfited me when I heard him say, 'Stop being good Christians; start following Jesus'!

The voice of Jesus in this promissory mood is compelling. In the most breathtaking of all the promises Jesus made, He pledges that *the Trinity will make its home with us* (14:23).

The Holy Spirit in His humility wills to be the 'go-between God', the bond of loving perfection, the medium of fellowship and communion. The Spirit completes the Trinitarian circle and opens the intimacy between Father and Son to us, inviting us, even in the all-too human 'meanwhile', to share in the communion of self-giving love.

The Trinity that gives hospitality *to* us at the cost of the cross, will by the priceless gift of the Spirit accept hospitality *from* us.

What a world of wonders Jesus opens up!

On the other side of His death, He will come to us on either side of our dying, and because He lives, we will live also with a share in the same quality of life He now enjoys!

14:25–26

We continue to reflect on the amazing legacy Jesus left when He bequeathed to us the Spirit as His crowning gift. On ascending to glory, His first request is: 'Father, send them the Spirit.'

The Holy Spirit, we recall, is another 'advocate' like Jesus. As Jesus is our advocate in heaven before the Father's throne, so the Spirit is our advocate on earth in the courtroom of the world. The Holy Spirit will act only in the name of, or on the authority of, Jesus. His mission is to argue the case for the truth as it is in Jesus. He will do this in us and through us. All that Jesus has said, initially so misunderstood by the disciples, will be made plain to them by the Spirit. The Holy Spirit does not bring startling unheard-of revelation – as some today suppose – but unveils the truth of Jesus' words 'by an unfolding of their significance for the new situation in which the disciples find themselves'.[20]

The Spirit thus acts as our advocate before a sceptical world, not merely by giving us peaceful feelings but by instructing us in truth. He is our teacher. None of the new insights He gives, the new powers He bestows or the new initiatives He launches, will ever be detached from the Father's loving will or will ever discredit the name of Jesus. The Holy Trinity acts in concert on our behalf.

So, as you seek to be a distinctive disciple of Jesus, at home or work, in weakness or under pressure, you can be assured of the Holy Spirit's total support.

14:27

What people leave behind in their last will and testament is usually their accumulated riches and possessions to be distributed as they direct. But Jesus left behind no material possessions, no bank account, no houses or land. His legacy was of an altogether different kind.

Chief among Jesus' bequests was His '*peace*'. 'Shalom' was the usual Jewish greeting and farewell, which no doubt had become a mere convention. But Jesus surely filled it with new meaning. His peace is different in kind and in the way it is given from anything the world has to offer.

Rome offered its own brand of 'peace'. The *pax Romana* was a glorified protection racket in which at the point of a sword the Romans maintained order throughout their empire while taxing their subjugated people punitively for the privilege of having Imperial troops garrisoned in their province! Some peace!

Jesus was born and lived in just such a country at such a time, one occupied by the emperor's legions. Though Rome's rule was usually unobtrusive it was all-pervasive.

Tension was in the air, with the local Roman authorities sensitive to any hint of rebellion that might disturb their enforced peace. The smooth political elite who ran Jerusalem kept an anxious peace with Rome by slippery compromise, fearing all the time an outbreak of anti-Roman hostility by hot-headed Jewish nationalists.

Jesus was caught up in this volatile atmosphere and – as we hear in our chosen text – is about to be crushed between its rival factions as they play their deadly power games.

Even apart from this climate of social unrest, the outward circumstances of Jesus' life were tumultuous. He knew constant intrusions on His privacy, felt drained by the demands of ministry. He faced and felt, as no one else could, the bleakness of sin and burden of need all round Him. He was misunderstood and on the receiving end of cutting criticism and unkind innuendo.

If He enjoyed peace, then it was a peace that did not depend on outward circumstances or absence of conflict. In fact His is a resilient peace that thrives in the midst of trouble. As W.E. Sangster said of it, 'Galilee in storm and Calvary in darkness set it off.'[21]

The serenity of Jesus is born of confidence in His Father's goodness, trust in His Father's sovereignty, and surrender to His Father's will. Nothing can touch that. This is not a temporary therapy; not a placebo to con the heart into being untroubled. This is the Messiah's peace, the shalom of God's kingdom established in the midst of strife. Jesus bequeaths this peace as a gift to His nervous disciples on the verge of His departure to dispel their fear.

It is a peace brokered by His blood in the death of the cross, a peace powerful enough to absorb violence and resilient enough to outstay evil and drain it of its energy.

Already, in His overcoming human life, He knows that the ruler of the world has no claim on Him (14:30).

His going to the Father will eventually bring us joy and bring us to faith (14:28–29).

All that is left for Him is to lovingly obey the Father's final orders. With this determination, He bids His disciples follow Him to the final showdown with evil (14:31).

CHAPTER FOUR

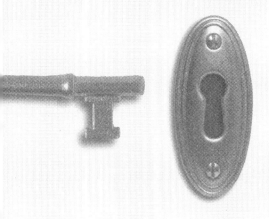

THE COMMUNITY OF FRIENDS

(John 15:1–25)

The Legacy of Jesus

His joy

JOHN 15:1-25

[1]'I am the true vine, and my Father is the gardener. [2]He cuts off every branch in me that bears no fruit, while every branch that does bear fruit he prunes so that it will be even more fruitful. [3]You are already clean because of the word I have spoken to you. [4]Remain in me, and I will remain in you. No branch can bear fruit by itself; it must remain in the vine. Neither can you bear fruit unless you remain in me.

[5]'I am the vine; you are the branches. If a man remains in me and I in him, he will bear much fruit; apart from me you can do nothing. [6]If anyone does not remain in me, he is like a branch that is thrown away and withers; such branches are picked up, thrown into the fire and burned. [7]If you remain in me and my words remain in you, ask whatever you wish, and it will be given you. [8]This is to my Father's glory, that you bear much fruit, showing yourselves to be my disciples.

[9]'As the Father has loved me, so have I loved you. Now remain in my love. [10]If you obey my commands, you will remain in my love, just as I have obeyed my Father's commands and remain in his love. [11]I have told you this so that my joy may be in you and that your joy may be complete. [12]My command is this: Love each other as I have loved you. [13]Greater love has no-one than this, that he lay down his life for his friends. [14]You are my friends if you do what I command. [15]I no longer call you servants, because a servant does not know his master's business. Instead, I have called you friends, for everything that I learned from my Father I have made known to you. [16]You did not choose me, but I

chose you and appointed you to go and bear fruit – fruit that will last. Then the Father will give you whatever you ask in my name. [17]This is my command: Love each other.

[18]'If the world hates you, keep in mind that it hated me first. [19]If you belonged to the world, it would love you as its own. As it is, you do not belong to the world, but I have chosen you out of the world. That is why the world hates you. [20]Remember the words I spoke to you: "No servant is greater than his master." If they persecuted me, they will persecute you also. If they obeyed my teaching, they will obey yours also. [21]They will treat you this way because of my name, for they do not know the One who sent me. [22]If I had not come and spoken to them, they would not be guilty of sin. Now, however, they have no excuse for their sin. [23]He who hates me hates my Father as well. [24]If I had not done among them what no-one else did, they would not be guilty of sin. But now they have seen these miracles, and yet they have hated both me and my Father. [25]But this is to fulfil what is written in their Law: "They hated me without reason."'

To avid TV audiences in the 1990s, *Friends* meant only one thing: the American soap opera about a bunch of attractive, footloose, Peter-Panish 'thirty somethings' sharing adjoining apartments in New York.

Friends was slick, witty and engaging, even if its characters were vacuous and amoral. It was seen by some as a parable of our postmodern times where friendship offers a surrogate family. The theme song of the series, *I'll be there for you* ... became a popular mantra, well suited to a touchy-feely culture.

Jesus says to His followers: 'You are my friends.' And this is where the surprises start.

If His peace is not 'as the world gives ...' then His friendship is 'not as the world gives' either!

This is not the country of Rachel and Ross, Monica, Chandler, Phoebe and Joey. For a start, reflecting the high value placed on friendship in the ancient world, Jesus 'raises the stakes' so that the mantra 'I'll be there for you ...' gets a scary makeover as 'I will die for you ...': *'Greater love has no-one than this, that he lay down his life for his friends'* (15:13).

Because of the death of the one friend, the disciples become friends forever.

And what about how we find our friends?

My wife has a coffee mug given to her by her sister with the logo: 'Sisters by birth; friends by choice'. It's a nice sentiment, and in Mary and Annie's case, a true one. But when it comes to friendship with Jesus, the choice is not ours. *'You did not choose me, but I chose you ...'* (15:16).

He chooses *us* to be friends with Him and, by implication, to be friends with one another! The disciples didn't choose one another, and the Church would have been a less saving place if they had. For the friendship of Jesus was first extended to tax-gatherers and prodigals, and He welcomed sinners to His table. So civil servants like Matthew and tough-talking business types like James and John, find themselves in the same company as potential revolutionaries like Simon the Zealot. Contemplatives start hanging out with activists. Freed from the tyranny of choice, a community of friends emerges, which is not a mere company of the like-minded in danger of becoming an introverted mutual admiration society.

Freed from the bias of choice, we can begin to like people we didn't immediately 'take to', to relish the mystery of strangers, and to love even former enemies.

Our differences diminish in the mutual joy of being called 'His friends'. Together, we learn to sing in different parts in closer harmony: 'What a friend we have in Jesus …'!

And what of the special freedom friends enjoy of opening their hearts to each other?

This too is amplified by Jesus and raised to another level altogether. '*I no longer call you servants, because a servant does not know his master's business. Instead, I have called you friends, for everything that I learned from my Father I have made known to you*' (15:15).

Unlike a servant who is kept in the dark, a friend shares your confidence, and is party to your private thoughts and plans. This can be burdensome.

Abraham was called the 'friend of God' not least because prior to bringing judgment on Sodom and Gomorrah, God posed Himself the question, 'Shall I hide from Abraham what I am about to do?' Abraham bears the burden of being God's friend and of sharing God's dark plans.

Abraham Heschel once said of Israel that, in receiving God's revelation, Israel had been chosen 'to dream the dreams of God'.[1] Now the followers of the Christ, the true Israel, are privileged as His friends, to know the truth, to share the saving secrets of the kingdom, in short, to be made privy to everything the Father has told Him!

All this is to say that the community of friends are *His* friends first. C.S. Lewis famously noted that where lovers walk towards each other, friends walk beside each other towards the shared object of their interest. Jesus is our shared interest, our consuming interest. More than that He is our shared life. We are the community of His friends because we are a *root* community. We are rooted in Him by His choice and we remain attached to Him by loving and obeying Him (14:15; 15:14). We are nourished by the same love with which the Father loves the Son (15:9) to love one another.

Our deep-rooted attachment to Him is the source of our life and love for one another. In short, we are branches in a vine through which flows the sap of God's own life and self-giving love.

In Craig Koester's words, 'the vine and its branches constitute a community of friends'.[2]

15:1–8 'I AM THE VINE ...'

The impressive symbolic action of foot washing is now matched by the vivid symbolic image of the vine and its branches.

The first and perhaps most pertinent thing to be said is that, 'I am the vine ...' is a very Israel-specific image.

Psalm 80 is typical of several passages in the Old Testament which speak of Israel as a vine planted in the land, on ground God had cleared by driving out the nations in Canaan (Psa. 80:8–9). The psalmist laments Israel's current condition in exile, ravaged and decimated like a plundered and ruined vineyard (80:12–13,16), and prays for her restoration. Mixing his metaphors, the singer speaks of God's vine as the root God has planted and the son He has raised up.

Isaiah, in trenchant prophetic language, mourns the fruitlessness of God's vineyard, Israel, which disappoints its owner (Isa. 5). The vineyard is judged for having failed to produce fruits of social justice and righteousness, and for bearing violence and oppression instead!

This is the highly charged political context in which Jesus makes such provocative statements as this, albeit here within the privacy of friendship.

Jesus has come as the true planting of the Lord. By falling into the ground and dying, He will take root and spring up with new life to bear fruit and to fulfil the destiny and mission of His people, Israel!

Viewed in this light, the image encapsulates the unique identity of Jesus and the ultimate challenge He poses to the nation and to its own complacent sense of security. 'I am the true vine, and my Father is the vine-dresser ... you are the branches' (15:1,5, ESV).

From now on, in Gary Burge's words, 'God's people are defined not as a people now planted in the vineyard of Israel, but as a people attached to Jesus'.[3]

The aim of the replacement planting and renewed capacity for fruit-bearing is that the Father may receive the glory due to His name (15:8).

What brings Him glory is a vine that bears fruit. This is achieved in two ways.

Firstly, by the 'pruning' done by the Father Himself.

He *clears out* dead and unfruitful branches (15:2,6).

He *cleans up* fruitful branches to make them even more productive (15:2b–3).

Since this cleaning process is already underway by what Jesus has said to them, we can assume that it will be maintained by the application to us of the sharp edge of God's living Word.

Secondly, this is achieved by the branches 'remaining' or 'abiding' in the vine (15:5). The language of 'abiding' implies conscious dependency and deliberately renewed attachment to Him, done in the awareness that 'apart from me you can do nothing'.

So we will abide …

- by remaining in the experienced good of His and the Father's love to us (15:4,9–10)
- by continuing to embrace His words and so remaining obedient and prayerfully confident of receiving the Father's gifts (15:7,10)
- by continuing to love one another (15:12,17).

Through our attachment to the vitality of the vine, the Father gets fruit and glory, and we get fruit-bearing branches, joy from Jesus to the fullest measure (15:8,11).

We pause to reflect on the *legacy of joy* that Jesus bequeathed to us.

He gives us His joy.

We rightly reverence Jesus as a 'man of sorrows, acquainted with grief' (Isa. 53:3, ESV). We need also to relish Jesus as a man of gladness, 'anointed with the oil of joy' above His companions (Heb.1:9).

Joy as He knew it is His deep delight in knowing that His Father loved Him and approved of Him. Joy was His profound satisfaction at faithfully doing the Father's will, even when anticipated as the fruit of His cross (Heb. 12:2).

He was jubilant at the defeat of evil (Luke 10:21) especially when it was achieved by the tentative efforts of trainee disciples.

Anticipating His later words (John 16:20–24), we relish a joy that does not synchronise with the world's prevailing moods; a joy that irresistibly seeks and finds us through pain, an undying joy that steps out to meet us on the other side of death, the fulsome joy found in His risen presence.

His joy is a resilient cheerfulness that no prison cell can suppress (Phil. 1:18–19).

His joy is an irrepressible confidence even when going through severe 'trials' (James 1:2).

In 15:11 Jesus explicitly connects joy with bearing fruit.

When Augustine reflected on how his conversion had rescued him from his desperate misspent pre-Christian quest for happiness, he wrote: 'How sweet all at once it was for me to be rid of those *fruitless joys* which I had once feared to lose! *You drove them from me,* you who are the true, the *sovereign joy* … You drove them from me and took their place.'[4]

Sovereign joy spoils us for lesser joys. 'Or,' as John Piper asks, are we in bondage to the pleasures of this world, so that, for all our talk about the glory of God, we love television and food and sleep and sex and money and human praise just like everybody else? If so, let us repent and fix our faces like flint toward the Word of God. And let us pray: O Lord, open my eyes to see the sovereign sight that in your presence is fullness of joy and at your right hand are pleasures for evermore (Psa. 16:11).[5]

His is the joy that remains (16:22). It is those who enjoy 'Amazing Grace' who appreciate that

Solid joys and lasting treasure,
None but Zion's children know.
                    John Newton

This is His legacy of lasting joy.

Joy is a fruit grown on the vine which is Jesus. Among recent commentators, Gary Burge in particular presses home the radical implications of Jesus' self-definition as the vine.

Does Jesus being the vine, he asks, call into question Israel's historic and still fiercely contested reliance on the Land for its identity?

Throughout his Gospel, John shows us a Jesus who fulfils the divine intention for all of Israel's feasts and institutions, including Passover and the Temple. Does the same principle apply to the Land itself?

This is Burge's verdict:

> Jesus is here revising Israel's theological assumptions about territory and religion. He is changing the place of rootedness for the people of God ...
>
> Jesus is the Vine and attachment to God comes through attachment to him. It is no longer a matter of possessing the vineyard; it is now a matter of knowing the one true vine.

Burge goes on to say: 'Jesus is thus pointing away from the vineyard as place, as territory of hills and valleys, cisterns and streams. In a word, Jesus spiritualises the land. He replaces the image of the vine and the promise of the land held so sacred in Judaism.'[6]

I believe the Western evangelical Church needs to hear this as a prophetic counter-balance to the almost total and uncritical support it gives to Zionism and the military policies of the present State of Israel.

At the very least it should renew a long-neglected concern for our fellow Christians in the Middle East, not least among the Palestinian people.

What an extraordinary new prospect would dawn for the Middle East if everyone stopped fighting over territory and trusted Jesus instead to make peace! The least we might do is occasionally encourage one another to hear the voice of the Palestinian Church as it tries to say just this – before it is crushed between the unyielding ideology of fanatical Islamic suicide bombers on the one side and the unrelenting weight of Israeli tanks on the other.

Listen to Gary Burge's conclusion:

> Just as Jesus is a replacement for the religious functions of
> the Temple, so too, Jesus replaces the religious inheritance
> of the Land. Jesus is the locus of God's habitation. He is the
> sole link to the vineyard, and to promote a vineyard without
> him, to promote a territorial salvation, is to miss entirely the
> thrust of his message about the Land.[7]

Worth pondering seriously, isn't it?[8]

15:9–17

As branches in the vine, we bear fruit in *loving one another* (15:9–12).

Jesus both models this self-giving love and makes it possible in us. This is part of His legacy – the command to love which He left behind as one of the 'standing orders' of His Church.

Although Jesus is secure in His Father's unqualified love and approval, He does not bask in that love in an indulgent way, oblivious to the responsibilities love enjoins. By keeping His Father's commands, Jesus has 'made himself at home in his love' (v.10, *The Message*). This loving eagerness to do the Father's will is a model for all believers. Even the Son of God learned the true cost of such obedience by what He was called upon to suffer. But the mutual love of Father and Son sustained His determination and sense of purpose. Love is proved by obedience. Not that our obedience earns His love as if 'his love is so sullen and miserly that it has to be wrenched from him by a kind of moral bribery' (Don Carson). No, love for Christ overflows in wanting to do His will.

This is not some grudging, dutiful allegiance.

Jesus finds supreme joy in this relationship of obedience to the Father. So can we find delight in doing His will and keeping His commands. Deepest joy is not dependent on passing moods or outward events but springs from unwavering commitment to Jesus Christ. No more miserable Christian exists than the one who is short-changing on obedience. Draw generously on His love, do His commands, and drink deep from the well of His lasting joy.

Such love then grows out of our attachment to Jesus. Apart from our relationship with Him we can do nothing and love no one. Loving like this is an outflow to one another of the love we receive and relish from the Father and the Son.

This is what the '*friends* of Jesus' do! Their love is a matter of obedience. Servants obey slavishly out of duty, but friends do what pleases the Master willingly and freely from the heart. His friends follow Him not with blind obedience but with eyes wide open to both the future glory and the cost of following Him because He has disclosed the Father's heart of love to them and let them into the secret of His deepest intentions.

Lesslie Newbigin points out that Jesus has spoken of His disciples earlier as servants (13:12–17) and will do so again (15:20). But, he writes, 'the master has done the work of a slave for them and therefore the relationship cannot be described simply as that of master and slave'. [9]

As we mentioned earlier, such friends enjoy the freedom of

being chosen. None of us has gate-crashed the 'friendship' between the Father and the Son but have been invited into it.

This should prevent us, as we saw, from complaining about the others Jesus has chosen, since He did not negotiate with us over whom He would choose to be His friends.

Being chosen can only enhance our sense of dignity and worth, deepening our assurance that His feelings towards us will not change.

To know we are chosen can save us from harmful introspection.

We can agree with Bruce Milne as he comments on this text that our standing in grace gives us massive encouragement. 'We go,' he writes, 'not because we are worthy or equipped or attractive or skilled or experienced, or in any way suitable and appropriate. We go because we have been summoned and sent.'[10]

And, we might add, summoned and sent by love to love (15:17).

'See, how these Christians love one another' is what the pagans said wonderingly about the Early Church. May it be said of us.

15:18-25

It is a sad fact but one to be faced realistically, that friendship with Jesus will almost invariably attract the *hostility of the world.*

In being His friends, bearing the burden of the truth He had entrusted to them, the disciples put their lives on the line for His sake. Even Peter initially buckled under the pressure and denied the bond of friendship.

When we have to choose between truth and friendship, then

our integrity is tested. The trial of Jesus brought this to a head. Pilate was one of 'Caesar's friends', a group of associates with privileged access to the emperor. Though Pilate was convinced that Jesus was innocent, he feared that talk of Jesus being a king would upset Rome, and the baying crowd was only too ready to play on his fears: 'If you let this man go, you are no friend of Caesar. Anyone who claims to be a king opposes Caesar' (John 19:12).

A double tragedy ensued. 'Pilate abandoned the truth in order to maintain the friendship of the emperor on which his own career depended.'[11] Even more tragically and ironically, the Jews preferred the Senate's choice to God's choice of king to reign over them!

For the meantime, Jesus alone bears the full brunt of the world's hatred, whether it comes from Rome or Jerusalem. But in the future, His disciples will attract the same kind of hostility He faced, an inevitable consequence of following Him (15:19).

But why do Christ's followers face such opposition from the 'domination-system' of this present world-order?

Why are we opposed?
• *Because we no longer belong to the world-system (15:19)*
Rather we have been chosen 'out of the world'. Though we remain very much 'in it', we are not part of its distinct ethos (cf. 17:14–16).

As Kelly and Moloney explain, our 'differentness' attracts the world's hostility.

Because the followers of Jesus can no longer be complicit in the false peace built on idolatrous absolutes; because they are not one with the world in rejecting the Word that has come to it; because they have been called out of the self-serving concerns of worldly glory, they can expect no love from that quarter (15:19–20). The world's allergic reaction to the Word is the result of an idolatry bearing the distinctive fruits of murder and lies. [12]

Why are we opposed?
- *Because we are closely associated with Jesus (15:20–21).*

Although we are His friends, rather than merely His servants, we are not 'above' the fray where the Master suffers and endures.

The way the domination system treated Him is the way it will regard us.

Since it did not recognise Him, it will not acknowledge us (v.21).

As that strange and saintly seventeenth-century Scotsman, Samuel Rutherford, wrote in his incarceration: 'God has called you to Christ's side, and the wind is now in Christ's face in this land; and since you are with him you cannot expect the sheltered or sunny side of the hill.' [13]

Why are we opposed?
- *Because the truth of Jesus which His followers will represent exposes the evil of the world system (15:22).*

The coming of the light has shown up the darkness of the world. His gracious words of life and truth have revealed the deadly lies and deceit at the heart of the world's propaganda. His miracles of healing and deliverance have threatened the 'unlove' and oppression ruling the world.

Jesus is hated for it, and with Him, the Father.

There is now no excuse for the world. Light has come. Truth has come. Salvation has come. To turn against this saving revelation and to resist this saving invitation is to seek to kill God.

There is a blind irrationality to the world's hatred of God but we may take comfort from the fact that Scripture already forewarns us of the hostility we will face as Christ's followers (15:25). This fact alone will sustain us. But, thankfully, we are soon to learn that we are far from alone in our conflict with the world.

CHAPTER FIVE

THE ADVOCACY
OF THE TRUTH

(John 15:26–16:33)

The Legacy of Jesus

His witnesses

JOHN 15:26-16:33

26'When the Counsellor comes, whom I will send to you from the Father, the Spirit of truth who goes out from the Father, he will testify about me. 27And you also must testify, for you have been with me from the beginning.

John 16

1'All this I have told you so that you will not go astray. 2They will put you out of the synagogue; in fact, a time is coming when anyone who kills you will think he is offering a service to God. 3They will do such things because they have not known the Father or me. 4I have told you this, so that when the time comes you will remember that I warned you. I did not tell you this at first because I was with you.

5'Now I am going to him who sent me, yet none of you asks me, "Where are you going?" 6Because I have said these things, you are filled with grief. 7But I tell you the truth: It is for your good that I am going away. Unless I go away, the Counsellor will not come to you; but if I go, I will send him to you. 8When he comes, he will convict the world of guilt in regard to sin and righteousness and judgment: 9in regard to sin, because men do not believe in me; 10in regard to righteousness, because I am going to the Father, where you can see me no longer; 11and in regard to judgment, because the prince of this world now stands condemned.

12'I have much more to say to you, more than you can now bear. 13But when he, the Spirit of truth, comes, he will guide you into all truth. He will not speak on his own; he will speak only what he hears, and he will tell you what is yet to come. [14]He will bring glory to me by taking from what is mine and making it known to you. [15]All that belongs to the Father is mine. That is why I said the Spirit will take from what is mine and make it known to you.

[16]'In a little while you will see me no more, and then after a little while you will see me.'

[17]Some of his disciples said to one another, 'What does he mean by saying, "In a little while you will see me no more, and then after a little while you will see me," and "Because I am going to the Father"?' [18]They kept asking, 'What does he mean by "a little while"? We don't understand what he is saying.'

[19]Jesus saw that they wanted to ask him about this, so he said to them, 'Are you asking one another what I meant when I said, "In a little while you will see me no more, and then after a little while you will see me"? [20]I tell you the truth, you will weep and mourn while the world rejoices. You will grieve, but your grief will turn to joy. [21]A woman giving birth to a child has pain because her time has come; but when her baby is born she forgets the anguish because of her joy that a child is born into the world. [22]So with you: Now is your time of grief, but I will see you again and you will rejoice, and no-one will take away your joy. [23]In that day you will no longer ask me anything. I tell you the truth, my Father will give you whatever you ask in my name. [24]Until

now you have not asked for anything in my name. Ask and you will receive, and your joy will be complete.

[25]'Though I have been speaking figuratively, a time is coming when I will no longer use this kind of language but will tell you plainly about my Father. [26]In that day you will ask in my name. I am not saying that I will ask the Father on your behalf. [27]No, the Father himself loves you because you have loved me and have believed that I came from God. [28]I came from the Father and entered the world; now I am leaving the world and going back to the Father.'

[29]Then Jesus' disciples said, 'Now you are speaking clearly and without figures of speech. [30]Now we can see that you know all things and that you do not even need to have anyone ask you questions. This makes us believe that you came from God.'

[31]'You believe at last!' Jesus answered. [32]'But a time is coming, and has come, when you will be scattered, each to his own home. You will leave me all alone. Yet I am not alone, for my Father is with me.

[33]'I have told you these things, so that in me you may have peace. In this world you will have trouble. But take heart! I have overcome the world.'

15:26–16:4

There is a scene in the first of the *Matrix* trilogy of films which grabbed my attention when I first saw it in a cinema in Nashville. The hero, a computer geek who unwittingly breaks through to another level of reality, showing fear and uncertainty, is faced with making a choice between two pills, one red, the other blue.

Opposite him sits a tall black man, dressed all in black, whose name is Morpheus, and who conveys an aura of authority. He sympathises with his visitor, guessing that he feels lost, feels that, like Alice, he had tumbled down a deep rabbit hole.

You are here, Morpheus tells the young man, because deep down and all along, like a 'splinter in the mind', you've suspected that all is not right with the world.

The conversation continues:

Morpheus: Do you know what I'm talking about?

Neo: The Matrix?

Morpheus: Do you want to know what it is?

Neo nods his assent.

Morpheus: The Matrix is everywhere … you can see it when you look out of your window, when you turn on your television. You can feel it when you go to work, when you go to church, when you pay your taxes. It is the world that has been pulled over your eyes to blind you from the truth …

Neo: What truth?

Morpheus: That you are a slave …

Morpheus then holds out his hands. In each palm is a capsule, one red the other blue. He is offering the younger man a chance of the truth.

Morpheus: … you take the blue pill – the story ends, you wake up in your bed and you believe … whatever you want to believe. You take the red pill – you stay in Wonderland

and I show you how deep the rabbit hole goes ...

The film is a strange mixture of New Age spiritualities and religious ideas, but at this one point, it was turned into gospel. I was riveted, knowing that the film had touched the central issue of our time: *What is truth?*

Jesus has already spoken of the unreasoning way in which evil contests truth in the world as we know it. No one, He points out, who knows Scripture, should be at all surprised by this (15:25).

To be forewarned, they say, is to be forearmed. So Jesus warns His disciples of the unremitting hostility the world will show towards them. It will be ruthless and may even lead to death. The opposition will be all the more bitter for being done for religious reasons. Here, the anticipated rejection by the synagogue may reflect the actual situation faced by John's readers towards the end of the first century when a threatened and defensive Judaism reacted to the threat to its own existence by closing ranks and seeking its scapegoats. So, tragically, at this crucial time, fear and unbelief place God's first-chosen people in the camp of the 'world' that hates the Messiah and His followers!

So, if His words are heeded, no one will be surprised by the hostile reception they face for being faithful to His name.

The Lutheran pastor, Dietrich Bonhoeffer, spoke truly when he wrote of the 'cost of discipleship'. Bonhoeffer himself 'took the red pill' and paid the price in laying down his life, martyred by the Nazi regime in Germany, a particularly brutal form of the domination system.

As Amy Carmichael wrote,

No wound? No scar?
Yet, as the Master shall the servant be,
And pierced are the feet that follow Me;
But thine are whole; can he have followed far
Who has nor wound nor scar.

When, as a callow youth, I quoted Carmichael's words to a congregation, I was taken to task by a solid citizen of the church who accused me of hyperbole and of being overly dramatic.

Perhaps he was right. I was probably being pretentious. My wounds have been mere scratches, long since healed over and leaving no scar.

But for many Christians throughout history the hatred of the world's system has not been hyperbole but harsh reality. In the twentieth century alone, it is estimated there have been over 25 million martyrs for Jesus in places as far apart as China, Soviet Russia, Cambodia, Africa and South America, and many others.

Let's recall the courtroom motif that has shaped our view of John's account so far.

As disciples of Jesus we are inevitably caught up in the tense and often painful trial of truth going on in the nations.

We noted earlier how God once challenged Israel through the prophet Isaiah to stand up and be counted as His witnesses in the courtroom of the nations who are mocking God's claims to be the one Creator and Lord. Only Israel could verify this by giving her testimony.

Now in a tragic reversal of the situation, it is God's own people who are sceptical about the claims and identity of the One whom

God has sent, so that Jesus is effectively put on trial. He looks to His disciples to testify in His defence, for they have been with Him 'from the beginning' and will be able to tell the whole story.

So we too are called to be His witnesses, not as those who were there at the beginning, but in our own time able to add our voices and lives to those who were there in the ongoing witness to the wonder of Jesus. But notice we are not alone as we face the world's hatred and seek to bear witness to the truth.

The Holy Spirit is sent by Jesus from the Father as the Spirit of truth who goes out from the Father (15:26). The rich phrases piled one on another reveal that the resources of the whole Trinity are being committed at this point to this end.

Such provision comes home to our hearts and resounds in our experience in the Person of the Holy Spirit who again stands alongside us as our friend at court and advocate for the truth.

Kelly and Moloney say, of the role the Spirit will play, that 'this other, divinely-given defender will be a permanent counterpoise to the unrelenting opposition the disciples will suffer at the hands of this world and its ruler'.[1]

Savour that statement: '... a *permanent counterpoise* to the unrelenting opposition the disciples will suffer ...'

And not only are we not alone in witnessing to the truth, but we are not even the leading counsel. The Holy Spirit is the chief witness for Jesus. We are merely asked to join our testimony to His and in support of His.

Once again – as with Jesus and the Father – the Deuteronomic requirement of two witnesses, in this case His disciples *and* the Holy Spirit, is upheld as the means to establish truth.

The empowering comfort and advocacy of the Holy Spirit is promised to sustain us in bearing witness to the true identity of Jesus as the incarnate Son of God, the one Saviour and Lord of all.

No disciple of Jesus ever witnesses alone or unaided. We are not meant to be passive but we can take heart from being constantly reminded of what someone has called 'the *senior partnership of the Holy Spirit*'.

What a consolation this is.

16:7–11

Don't let's forget the situation facing the disciples as they contemplate Christ leaving them.

His way ahead seems to be a dead-end; His voice will soon, it seems, be silenced forever; His truth appears on the verge of being discredited, His cause deemed a humiliating failure …

Perhaps they feel – as John's readers may now be feeling – that the world system that threatens and rejects and expels with violence, sometimes even for religious reasons, is more real and more powerful than the intangible fellowship of Father and Son.

Jesus, however, turns His leaving to their advantage: It is good that I go away so that the Holy Spirit may come!

Bruce Milne comments well. 'The crucial phrase is "go away". This is not so much a spatial movement as a spiritual exaltation. Jesus will now "go away" through death and resurrection to the glory of the Father's presence …'[2]

It is this whole movement of victory through suffering that

makes possible the coming of the Spirit.

Milne continues: 'The ministry of the Spirit is not a vague impartation of spiritual energy, but the specific ministry of proclaiming and applying to the disciple community, the triumphant procession of Jesus through death and resurrection to the right hand of the Father.'[3]

It is in this way that – to anticipate – the Spirit will always glorify Jesus (16:15).

Why is the Holy Spirit given?

Jesus has shown the disciples that the Holy Spirit will act as the 'counsel for the defence' as they bear witness to Him. Now we learn that, as Christ's followers bear witness to the truth about Him, the Spirit will act towards the world as *counsel for the prosecution*.

The Spirit will disturb the world's complacent self-satisfaction, and shatter the world's cherished illusions.

In Kelly and Moloney's words, the world 'will be identified as a web of violence and idolatrous untruth, in allergic reaction to the non-violent, life-giving truth of the love offered it'.[4]

Acting through the disciples, the Spirit will convict the world and turn its valuation of God and Jesus and the disciples upside down.

The word 'convict' (*elencho*) construes the mission of the Spirit to be the announcement of the verdict of God in the cosmic trial. The great missiologist, J.H. Bavinck, coined the term 'elenctics' for this activity. The prophetic challenge of all mission work, Bavinck suggested, is to ask of every culture: 'What have you done with God?'[5]

The Spirit will convict the world of *sin*

The sin – contrary to some popular preaching – is not that of not believing in Jesus. Rather, by refusing to believe in Jesus, the world's deep unbelief is radically exposed. 'The world will be convicted of sin because those who belong to it do not believe in Jesus' (Andrew Lincoln, p.119).

Rejecting Jesus leaves you in your sin without a Saviour.

The Spirit will convict the world of *righteousness*

The righteousness in question is that of Jesus.

As Andrew Lincoln explains,

> The Paraclete will convict the world of the righteousness of the One it has condemned to death and of the justice of the cross. He has been vindicated by the divine judge in the trial, and the Paraclete can drive home this verdict because Jesus' departure to a realm where he is no longer visible to the disciples constitutes his glorification, the divine seal of approval on his death.[6]

So the world's verdict of death passed on Jesus will be reversed by the verdict of life issued by His resurrection which justifies Him and us with Him, and is confirmed by His ascension to the Father which will be His total vindication.

The Spirit will convict the world of *judgment* because the ruler of the domination system is judged and deposed at the cross (cf. 12:31ff.)

The Spirit will reveal that it is the world and its ruler, not Jesus, its true Lord, who has been discredited in the events of Easter.

What an amazing turn of events this is! It amounts to a total reversal of values and verdicts, now to be announced through the witness of the Spirit-empowered disciples.

No wonder it is to our advantage that Jesus goes back to the Father. Because He does, the Spirit comes and everything looks different to Spirit-filled eyes.

What an intense relief it is to realise that we are not the judge: matters of final judgment can safely be left in His hands alone. Nor, we may be pleased to learn, are we called to be the prosecuting counsel, as if we had to convince the world of the rightness of Jesus' cause.

We are not asked to have answers to all the questions thrown at us but only to do what a witness does best, which is to say what she or he has seen and heard. Thanks be to God that it is the Spirit's work to convince the world of God's truth. Ours is to be faithful in bearing our testimony.

But the implications for the Church's witness and preaching are clear.

What we proclaim is not a better product than others are touting as the recipe for a more fulfilled life; we are declaring the crisis of the world. Our proclamation is a prophetic exposure of the domination system, of its moral and spiritual bankruptcy.

We declare the invalidity of the world's values and standards, and a reversal of its verdict on God and Jesus. And a Church committed to the advocacy of truth in the power of the Spirit will be a Church that refuses to conform to the world. It will be a Church dedicated to the renewal of its mind by a courageous standing aside from the social consensus and the prevailing cultural ideologies.

In this sense the Church has to be against the world in order truly to be for the world.

Craig Koester accurately summarises the stance of John's Gospel when he says:

> The community's distinction from the world was the basis for their engagement with the world. A religion that is the warp of the social fabric cannot easily confront society with its flaws. It is precisely because the community was different from the world that it could challenge the world on the basis of the love and Word of God.[7]

16:12–15

The Spirit comes when Jesus leaves.

The Spirit continues where Jesus leaves off.

'*I have many things to say to you, but you cannot bear them now …*' (ESV)

The Spirit, like Jesus (cf. 14:10) does not speak on His own authority, but speaks what He hears.

The Spirit will declare all that Jesus has which is all that the Father has.

The Holy Spirit will not only reiterate what Jesus has said, stirring us up by way of reminder; He will also enlighten us about what Jesus wills in the future by way of further revelation.

'All truth' here is not truth about everything and anything, nuclear physics for example! Rather, the Spirit will lead us into all the truth we need to know about God and our relationship with Him as it is embodied in Jesus who is 'Truth'.

In other words, here is a promise of ongoing guidance in all that it means to be a disciple of Jesus Christ. Through the Spirit, Jesus will continue to speak and act after the ascension.

When the Spirit comes (to unleash the momentum so graphically described in the Acts of the Apostles), He will lead the Church into all truth about Father and Son (the unfolding revelation of Jesus such as we find in the New Testament letters and Gospels), and He will declare what is to come (the prophetic and eschatological vision of God's future which culminates in the book of Revelation).

Luke begins the Acts of the Apostles by recalling his Gospel in which was described what Jesus *began* to do and to teach until His ascension. Clearly the ongoing work of the ascended Jesus is carried on through His authorised agents who are led and taught and energised by the Spirit.

The New Testament letters were once described as 'the posthumous epistles of the ascended Lord'. Jesus never wrote a book but He left us Spirit-filled witnesses who did.

Because Jesus and the Spirit are at one, nothing the Spirit subsequently reveals will contradict the historic testimony to Jesus contained here in the Gospels. 'What is to come' will be made known to us but it will be a further unfolding of the significance of what has already and majestically come to us in the Jesus who lived and died and rose again. Father, Son and Spirit share a common life and act in perfect harmony. One way to measure what purports to be the work of the Holy Spirit is to note carefully what it shows us of Jesus.

It is the mission of the Spirit to *glorify* Jesus (16:15). This could hardly be otherwise since His coming is attendant on the going of Jesus to the Father in His ascension and exaltation. So when the Spirit is given from the throne of God, He comes trailing clouds of glory that gather round Christ

- revealing to us the lordship of Jesus (Acts 2:26)
- reproducing in us the character of Jesus (Gal. 5)
- releasing among us the powers and gifts of the ascended Christ
- reviving in our hearts the self-giving love of Christ.

One of the many merits of John Taylor's classic study of the Holy Spirit – *The Go-Between God* – is that he shows the link between power and perception.

Most noticeably in Luke–Acts, the Holy Spirit is usually associated with *power*, albeit the power to achieve moral and spiritual ends. In John however – and to a similar extent in Paul's writings – the Spirit is more often associated with *perception*, with the giving of illumination and knowledge.

Taylor helpfully connects the two aspects of the Spirit's work. The Spirit, he writes, '... enables us, not by making us supernaturally strong, but by opening our eyes.'[8]

So the Holy Spirit leads us further into the truth by giving us a clearer view of the glory of Christ. This suggests an education of the vision and desire of the heart for which Paul's Ephesian prayer (Eph.1:17–23) is a perfect plea.

The Holy Spirit, then, does not intend to draw attention to Himself by needless gimmicks but works wonders that glorify Jesus. He acts and behaves in ways which lead us to conclude: that's what Jesus does and that's the way Jesus does it. The Holy Spirit exemplifies the divine humility in turning the spotlight away from Himself and onto Jesus. In Jim Packer's words, the Holy Spirit 'is the hidden spotlight shining on the Saviour'.[9]

> Thank you O my Father,
> For giving us your Son,
> And leaving your Spirit,
> till the work on earth is done.
> Melody Green

16:16–33

If 16:1–15 speaks of the gift of the Spirit on the other side of Pentecost, so 16:16–33 speaks of the gift of the Son on the other side of Easter.

First, the promise is of *Jesus' personal presence*, 16:16–22.

The disciples are puzzled by His talk of 'a little while ...' and His promise 'I will see you again ...'

What can He mean?

With John's hindsight, it now seems clear that Jesus is referring to His resurrection appearances. They will wait a little while but then He will see them again beyond death!

But the 'little while' will seem an agonising wait. Their sorrow and grief will be real and deep (16:20). They will 'weep and lament', he says, over the loss of His personal friendship, the loss of His clear commands and instruction, the loss of His comforting presence.

They had left all to follow Him; now without Him they would lose everything. The dashing of their hopes and dreams would be made more bitter by the world's rejoicing over His death. It would rub salt in a deep wound to see violence victorious, evil exultant, and His enemies gloating over His demise.

But He insists *you will see me again …*'

Some people find it easy to explain why Jesus spoke in this positive way; after all, He was divine and omniscient and knew in advance with cold clarity how things were going to work out. But I cannot see how this fits the picture John gives of a heart deeply troubled by what He was about to face. To imagine that Jesus simply looked past the suffering in some mechanical way, as if it didn't really register with Him because He knew the outcome, robs Him of his humanness and puts Him at a damaging distance from us.

No, His confidence is born of communion with His Father. It is not a product of omniscience but a statement of trust. Jesus offers His disciples a share in the certainty of His own faith: '*you will see me again …*'

When He appeared to them as the Risen Lord, John records, they rejoiced because they had 'seen the Lord' (John 20:18,20,25, 27–29).

The pain of enduring the 'little while …' will be worth it, He assures them, just as a mother suffers the pains of pregnancy and childbirth for the joy set before her of holding the baby in her arms (16:21).

The imagery Jesus uses here may well have deep Old Testament resonances, reminding us of the scale of what is happening to Him. In particular, Isaiah (Isa. 26:16–21), speaks an oracle in which all three themes – a little while, birth pangs and the possibility of resurrection – occur together. The prophet is voicing the anguished cry of an Israel desperately needing rebirth. This is just what Jesus' 'going to the Father' will accomplish for Israel – the dying and remaking of the people of God in His own death and resurrection. So, on Easter Sunday, will a 'country be born in a day' (Isa. 66:8).

But, whatever the nuances in Jesus' words, for the disciples then, John's readers later and for us today, the need is for more immediate consolation.

Austin Farrer recalls the story of a solid country doctor summoned to attend a squire's wife who was in labour. After the birth, still feeling only half-alive, she moaned that the suffering was unbearable and pressed him as to why it was all so painful. The good doctor, dutifully but unimaginatively, launched on a longwinded, philosophical and physiological justification for her pain. She interrupted him: 'It hurts just the same ...' At that moment the midwife brought the baby back into the room and laid him in his mother's arms. And suddenly the woman began to think of how it would be when she suckled him and suddenly, as Farrer puts it, she remembered no more the anguish for her joy of that little man who was born into the world.

Contemplating the mysterious suffering of the world as it is concentrated in the agony of the cross, we do not understand and are baffled and bemused. But we see Jesus again and we realise – in Farrer's words – that 'a Son is better than an explanation'. [10]

So it proved for the disciples.

What a stunning statement it is: '*Now is your time of grief, but I will see you again and you will rejoice, and no-one will take away your joy*' (16:22).

From our distance, we see Him again, of course, only through their eyes, as they give eye-witness accounts of the truth of His risenness – as John does right here in this very Gospel.

We see Him again – risen and alive – and our hearts rejoice. And if, like theirs, our joy is derived from His resurrection and sustained by His risenness, then nothing, not even death, can rob us of it (16:22).

16:23–33

Having promised His personal presence after a little while, Jesus now makes *provision for the disciples' future*.

Firstly, He promises that their *prayers* will be effective (16:23–24, 26). They need ask nothing of Him that the Father will not give them; they must ask nothing of the Father that they would not have asked of Jesus.

They must ask 'in His name'. His authority when invoked constrains our praying to what serves His best interests, while at the same time authorises our praying to ask for what He knows is in our best interest. Praying 'in His name' links us to all that He goes to the Father to secure for Himself and for us in the realm of glory and grace.

Since we love the Son, we honour His name; since we believe in the Son we have faith in His name, and so we pray. We are drawn into the loving relationship of Father and Son and so we pray.

'The Father himself loves you …' – what a profound and deeply enriching assurance! So when we pray 'in His name' we open up our lives to the Father's love.

Secondly, Jesus promises them some *plain speaking* (16:25).

Apparently, up to this point, Jesus has been speaking 'figuratively'. The word used, however, does not mean 'metaphorically' so much as 'enigmatically' or 'mysteriously' (cf. use of the word in 10:6). But the time is coming when all will be made clear. This is the 'hour' – that, as we have seen all along, signifies Jesus' passage to the Father.

A new era of revelation will begin with the coming of the Holy Spirit as teacher, revealer, enlightener and leader into all truth. The truth of God in Jesus encapsulated in the apostolic gospel is a '*mysterion*' but it is a revealed mystery, an open secret, made known by the agency of the Spirit to hearts awakened to His wisdom.

They seem to believe that the time for Him to speak plainly has already begun (v.29). But He responds ironically: '*You believe at last!*' (v.31).

What He tells them next is to the effect: if it's plain speaking you want, here it is! '… You will be scattered, each to his own home. You will leave me all alone …'

What a bitter and ironic truth that is! They have been concerned all along that *He* was leaving *them*, and leaving them alone!

Now He confronts them with the brutal truth that it is *they* who will desert *Him*!

- The world seeks to isolate Him and pick Him off. With His followers scattered by fear and intimidation, He stands alone. But He stands bravely in solitary defiance. Though His friends flee from Him and His enemies line up against Him, the Father is with Him and that is more than enough.
- The world seeks to invade His peace, to shatter His confidence, and to overrun the citadel of His heart where the Father's loving will holds Him secure. But the world fails to destroy His peace, and in the shelter of His unshakeable trust we too can find true rest.

'I have told you these things, so that in me you may have peace. In this world you will have trouble. But take heart! I have overcome the world' (16:33).

What an amazing reassurance this is.

Martin Luther wrote to his friend and fellow Reformer, Philip Melancthon, that 'such a saying as this is worthy to be carried from Rome to Jerusalem upon one's knees'!

What an extraordinary peace Jesus gives which can co-exist with pressure and even persecution! His peace stems from His victory over sin and evil. He has already overcome the world!

Once more, we realise that when Jesus speaks of peace He is not talking of some escapist fantasy, not some feel-good factor, enjoyable only in trouble-free times. This is not the peace of holidays and retreats but a peace to be experienced in the heat of battle. We can discover tranquillity in the middle of trials, calm in the centre of crises.

Such peace is the fruit of 'courage' ('take heart', NIV) – which was exactly what Jesus urged the disciples to display when caught in the storm on Galilee. Jesus does not promise His followers a bed of roses. In fact He foresees trouble ahead, inevitable conflict because we follow Him. But because He conquered, we take courage. Because He is victorious, we can be too.

The victory He wins, we remind ourselves, is on the largest possible scale.

What was conquered in the cross was not merely our private temptations, not our personal sins only.

What was judged and conquered was 'the world' construed as a 'godless principle'.

The 'world' with its false loves, false values, false ideas, false addictions ... the 'world' with its pretensions to domination, its spurious propaganda, its propensity to violence ... the 'world' in all its alienation from a good Creator, with its hostility to truth, corruption of righteousness and perversion of justice ... it is *this* world which He has conquered and overcome in the cross.

The world's hatred was drained out of it on the cross, no match for the love that God pours into the world.

'In Christ,' said P.T. Forsyth in his greatest book, 'the world passed its judgment on God, and Christ took it. But still more, in him God passed his judgment on the world, *and Christ took that also*'. [11]

The cross, Forsyth insists, only climaxes the victories Jesus has won all along.

He was dying and conquering all His life, in word and deed. He never failed to conquer at every crisis of thought or action. So, while living, and before He is crucified, He still says, 'I *have* overcome the world … and all the crises of His life had themselves a crisis in His death, where the victory and solution was won once and for all.

He did not cheer the disciples with the sanguine optimism of the good time coming. It was not a sanguine optimism, but an optimism of actual faith and conquest. It was not the hope of a conquering Messiah soon. 'He is here', was the Gospel. And so we are not hopeful that the world will be overcome; we know it has. We are born into an overcome, a redeemed world.[12]

In his light we see light;
In his life we gain life;
In his victory we triumph.

Lesslie Newbigin is surely right in saying, 'The victory is wholly his. At the end, the triumph song of the Church will not be "We have overcome" but "Worthy is the Lamb who was slain."'[13]

So may we take fresh courage, sing our songs of faith, and by His Spirit bear witness to the truth.

CHAPTER SIX

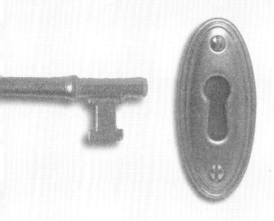

THE TRINITY OF LOVE

(John 17)

The Legacy of Jesus

His prayer

JOHN 17

¹After Jesus said this, he looked towards heaven and prayed:

'Father, the time has come. Glorify your Son, that your Son may glorify you. ²For you granted him authority over all people that he might give eternal life to all those you have given him. ³Now this is eternal life: that they may know you, the only true God, and Jesus Christ, whom you have sent. ⁴I have brought you glory on earth by completing the work you gave me to do. ⁵And now, Father, glorify me in your presence with the glory I had with you before the world began.

⁶'I have revealed you to those whom you gave me out of the world. They were yours; you gave them to me and they have obeyed your word. ⁷Now they know that everything you have given me comes from you. ⁸For I gave them the words you gave me and they accepted them. They knew with certainty that I came from you, and they believed that you sent me. ⁹I pray for them. I am not praying for the world, but for those you have given me, for they are yours. ¹⁰All I have is yours, and all you have is mine. And glory has come to me through them. ¹¹I will remain in the world no longer, but they are still in the world, and I am coming to you. Holy Father, protect them by the power of your name – the name you gave me – so that they may be one as we are one. ¹²While I was with

them, I protected them and kept them safe by that name you gave me. None has been lost except the one doomed to destruction so that Scripture would be fulfilled.

[13]'I am coming to you now, but I say these things while I am still in the world, so that they may have the full measure of my joy within them. [14]I have given them your word and the world has hated them, for they are not of the world any more than I am of the world. [15]My prayer is not that you take them out of the world but that you protect them from the evil one. [16]They are not of the world, even as I am not of it. [17]Sanctify them by the truth; your word is truth. [18]As you sent me into the world, I have sent them into the world. [19]For them I sanctify myself, that they too may be truly sanctified.

[20]'My prayer is not for them alone. I pray also for those who will believe in me through their message, [21]that all of them may be one, Father, just as you are in me and I am in you. May they also be in us so that the world may believe that you have sent me. [22]I have given them the glory that you gave me, that they may be one as we are one: [23]I in them and you in me. May they be brought to complete unity to let the world know that you sent me and have loved them even as you have loved me.

[24]'Father, I want those you have given me to be with me where I am, and to see my glory, the glory you have given me because you loved me before the creation of the world.

[25]'Righteous Father, though the world does not know you, I know you, and they know that you have sent me. [26]I have made you known to them, and will continue to make you known in order that the love you have for me may be in them and that I myself may be in them.'

When you come to this chapter of John's Gospel you really feel that you are walking on holy ground.

Here is recorded what for centuries has been called 'the high-priestly prayer of Jesus' though recent commentators prefer to call it His 'prayer of consecration'.

The prayer has three obvious sections:

- 17:1–5 to His *Father* for His own and His Father's glory
- 17:6–19 to His *Holy Father* for the disciples' unity, protection and sanctification
- 17:20–26 to His *Righteous Father* for the unity and glory of His future Church.

This 'Lord's Prayer' is a personalised and expanded form of the other 'Lord's Prayer'.

Jesus prays that His Father in heaven may be glorified ('*hallowed be your name …*'); that the work for which the Father gave Him kingly authority be successfully accomplished ('*your kingdom come, your will be done …*'); that His disciples be provided for, protected from evil and sanctified ('*give us … forgive us … deliver us from evil …*'); that His disciples be preserved as a unified community (… *as we forgive others* …') – and all once more to the glory of God ('… *for yours is the glory* …').

Not surprisingly,

17:1–5 JESUS PRAYS FIRST FOR HIS OWN AND HIS FATHER'S GLORY

We have noted that, strangely, unlike the Synoptic Gospels, the fourth evangelist does not mention the Transfiguration when Jesus became radiant with God's glory.

The omission is almost certainly deliberate, intended to stress that Jesus manifested His Father's glory at every turn of the road in everything He did. Jesus was not so much transfigured at one moment but translucent all the way through.

His life was one long doxology, lived to the praise of God's glory.

Now, in the critical 'hour' of rejection and humiliation, He prays that He may be valued and vindicated by the Father so that the Father may be acknowledged and honoured as never before.

Sharing John's resurrection hindsight, we can rejoice with Him that the events of Easter enhanced God's reputation as nothing before or since. The deep, dramatic action of God that wrought victory out of defeat, won glory out of shame, and birthed new creation out of death, eclipsed all the glories of the old creation.

As Isaac Watts taught us to sing,

Nature with open volume stands,
To spread her Maker's praise abroad;
And every labour of His hands

Shows something worthy of a God.

But in the grace that rescued man,
His brightest form of glory shines;
Here, on the cross, 'tis fairest drawn
In precious blood, and crimson lines.

Here once more is the saving paradox at the heart of the gospel narrative. Jesus will soon stand alone seemingly at the mercy of His enemies. But the climactic '*hour*' (17:1, ESV) which has now arrived is in the end not to be evil's finest hour but the Father's finest hour. The worst that evil will do masks the best that God will do.

The events now accelerating are not, as they appear to be, controlled by the evil powers waging war against God, but move under the Father's *sovereignty* and purpose. So Jesus prays as if His Father is the chief actor in the drama unfolding – which indeed He is. Judas, Caiaphas, Pilate – indeed the evil ruler of this world – have no claim on Jesus, and will serve as mere footnotes to the Easter story.

This is not, of course, how the disciples currently see or feel the situation. But they must surely have gained strength from overhearing His prayer (17:13).

The upward gaze of Jesus tells all: '… *he looked towards heaven and prayed* …' (17:1).

With His Father in the fatherly realm of heaven is where the real action is taking place. Jesus is moving in a larger orbit than His enemies will ever understand. They scurry around conspiring to trump up charges that will persuade others to do their dirty work for them; He refuses to panic and resorts to prayer, standing rocklike and still while the storm swirls around Him, trusting His Father to work for Him.

He then recalls thankfully the authority the Father had given Him to bestow eternal life on all flesh (17:2).

Armed with the Father's authority to judge, Jesus has pre-empted the last day, and upstaged the show trial about to arraign Him, by already bestowing a verdict of life on those who have believed (17:2 cf. 5:21–24).

Since this life which He always enjoys, is for Him a union of love and mutual giving, He can define it in no other way: '… *this is eternal life: that they may know you, the only true God, and Jesus Christ, whom you have sent*' (17:3).

Eternal life is not merely some spiritual adrenaline that makes the religious pulse race; not a kind of 'carbonated' version of the water of life we now have which gives it more fizz or sparkle or adds bubbles to our existing lifestyle. The life God is and offers is qualitatively different.

Eternal life is the gift of a relationship.

Eternal life is a personal share in the communion that is the Trinity, an introduction to the love which in the bond of the Spirit exists between Father and Son.

Jesus who is fully open to the Father opens Himself to us so that we can receive a measure of the life He shares with the Father.

So, His enemies must do what they will; He is concerned only that the work of ministry He has been given has already been accomplished. All that remains is for the Father to seal the Son's achievement as a 'finished work' by His crowning action in cross and resurrection.

What has been achieved 'on earth' is now to be matched by what will happen in the Father's 'presence'.

Seeing beyond the present crisis, Jesus prayerfully anticipates a resumption of the intimate relationship He enjoyed as a Son in the Father's heavenly presence. Jesus now prays that this glorious relationship – which is the unseen underlying ground of all reality, older than time, more foundational than creation itself – be recognised by those with eyes to see in our history and time.

So, like a solitary mountaineer at the peak of a summit, He strains His eyes into the distance to focus on the prize, on the joy set before Him, on the glory that awaits.

Secondly:

17:6–19 JESUS PRAYS FOR THE DISCIPLES' PROTECTION AND CONSECRATION

Movingly, Jesus describes the disciples as *those the Father has given Him* (17:2,6,9,20). Can this astonishing truth ever sink deep enough into us? We are the Father's gifts to His Son!

'If you, then, though you are evil, know how to give good gifts to your children, how much more will your Father … give good gifts to those who ask him!' (Matt. 7:11).

The privilege of being His disciple is to see oneself as part of the generous interchange between Father and Son. And in the mysterious interaction of divine initiative and human freedom, God's sovereign choice ('… those whom you gave me …') evokes a believing response ('they have kept your word … and received [the words you gave me] ...' 17:6,8, ESV).

The work that the Father had given to Him which Jesus has now done, is described in two ways.

'*I have manifested your name* ...' (17:6, ESV; strangely the NIV omits 'name'). Jesus is the self-expression of God. In His words and actions, God has revealed His essential character and shown His face. To have seen Jesus is to have seen the Father. Especially in the 'I am ...' discourses, we have been encouraged to hear the voice of God firsthand. Nothing deeper or more personal can be revealed about a person than that person's name; and Jesus has revealed God's name to us.

The disciples who believed this revelation now know the true secret of who Jesus is (17:7).

'... *I gave them the words you gave me* ...' (17:8).

The Word of God speaks only the words of God.

This does not mean that the Son is a mere ventriloquist's dummy, nor even that He is a prophetic mouthpiece as others had been before Him. Rather He speaks out of a unique union of heart and mind, a deep agreement of will and purpose with the Father. As a result His words are charged with 'spirit and life' (John 6:63), and constitute the final arbiter of human destiny (John 12:47–50).

The disciples have accepted His words, and so have grown even more sure that Jesus enjoys a unique relationship with God (17:8b).

Jesus now asks His Father to do three things for these disciples.

Firstly, *Keep them as a unified community* (17:11).

Let there be an end to divisiveness which is the devil's own business. Let there be no more Judas-like betrayal.

Keep and guard them, Father, as a shepherd looks after his sheep, and as I have done while I was with them.

'… protect them,' Jesus asks the Father, 'by the power of your name …' (17:11). This is the 'name you gave me' – that is, the entire revelation of God's essential nature and character that was entrusted to Jesus to display to the world. God's 'name' sums up all that God is. Within the fortress-like security of this mighty revelation, we take refuge.

By faith, we prove the Proverb true: '*The name of the LORD is a strong tower; the righteous run to it and are safe*' (Prov. 18:10).

Secondly, He prays,

'… *protect them from the evil one*' (17:15).

The followers of Jesus are emphatically 'not of the world', any more than Jesus was. They are not owned *by* and owe no allegiance *to* the prevailing domination system.

As the ruler of this world order had no claim on Him, so He prays that for them.

We may need to question whether we modern evangelicals take this prayer of Jesus seriously. We tend to pray for health and wealth and peace and job security and our children's future, and it's right to do so. But overhearing Jesus as He prays like this, should raise our level of awareness of the threat all around us. Listening in to His powerful pleading, should also surely encourage us, more often then we do, to resist the devil and all his wiles, in the prayerful authority of His strong name.

His prayer for them is summed up in the third request:

'*Sanctify them in the truth*' (17:17, ESV).

'Sanctify' – most scholars agree – would be better read as 'consecrate'. The emphasis here is not so much on moral cleanness – though that of course is implied – but on whole-hearted commitment to the Father's saving will.

'Sanctify them *in the truth* …' The disciples will be sanctified by their total immersion in the truth of the revelation Jesus has brought. This staggering, breathtaking truth, embodied in Jesus, captures our hearts, fires our imagination and romances us to the altar of sacrificial self-offering to make the consecration of love.

Jesus was consecrated and sent into the world by the Father (John 10:36). That is, Jesus was set apart for the Father's will and for the mission He was given.

Now, Jesus will both model this dedication for the disciples and by His utter self-offering to the Father's will make their dedication possible. '*For them I sanctify myself, that they too may be truly sanctified*' (17:19).

'Jesus is as determined to set himself apart for his Father's exclusive service as the Father is to set him apart.'[1] His consecration, like a whirlpool, sucks our consecration into His for the purpose of mission (17:18).

Milne comments:

> The gifts we exercise, the prayers we offer, the proclamation
> we share, the acts of compassion and mercy we endeavour,
> all flow from this primal moment in the shadow of Calvary
> as Jesus in prayer presents the mission of his church to
> the Father … Our work and witness, in all their variety,

are, already, in advance, gathered up, healed, renewed and perfected by being gathered into Jesus' holy response to the call of the Father …[2]

Significantly, in this second phase of His prayer, Jesus calls on God as '*Holy* Father' (17:11b, my italics). In praying for Himself, he calls on God simply as 'Father' (17:1), so evoking the love and intimacy of their relationship. Now in praying for the disciples, He invokes the *holiness of God, Holy Father*. It was Isaiah who characteristically described God as 'the Holy One of Israel'.

Holiness speaks of God's otherness, the sheer Godness of God that differentiates Him from all that He has made, that sets Him apart as utterly different from all else. Jesus invokes the power of the Father's holy name, to keep the disciples from all that would blur their distinctiveness as His people.

He prays that His Holy Father will protect them from the evil one who fuels the world's hatred of the disciples because they do not submit to its domination (17:14–15).

Jesus does not pray that we escape the tension of living in the world as it is. But He prays that while in it, we may be protected from evil, and kept whole and holy, fully dedicated to the gospel of the Son and the glory of the Father.

In the third and final section of this wonderful prayer:

17:20–26 JESUS PRAYS FOR THE UNITY AND GLORY OF HIS FUTURE CHURCH

In a remarkable leap of faith, Jesus projects into the future, envisioning many who will come to believe through the faithful witness of those He has just prayed for!

For them, His primary request is again '*that all of them may be one*' (17:21).

The oneness Jesus speaks of is the extraordinary and previously unrevealed unity that exists within the Trinitarian Godhead itself!

Jesus has made possible this unity by sharing with them something of His own glory and by opening them to the full mystery ('name') of the Trinitarian God (17:22).

Believers who inhabit this truth enjoy a unity modelled on the Trinity. Even more staggeringly, this unity is not only modelled on the Trinity but is in fact an actual participation in the life and love of the Trinity.

Then Jesus prays that those the Father has given Him will be with Him where He is to see His glory (17:24). What an extraordinary perspective this is! He looks forward to the very end of the story, the future glory of the finally accomplished work. And He wants us with Him!

Whatever heaven turns out to be scarcely matters as long as it means being 'with Him'. The ultimate prospect is to 'see His glory'.

We can say with John, as we contemplate the wonders of Christ's earthly ministry, sacrificial death and stupendous resurrection, 'The Word became flesh and made his dwelling among us. We have seen his glory …' But there is a glory of Jesus we have not yet seen, one He had before the world was made, and will have again.

And we shall see *that* glory!

We shall see what heaven sees, and see Him as heaven sees Him.

We shall see Him radiant with the outshining of His original divine splendour; we shall see Him resplendent with the honour and majesty He has accrued by His incarnation and victory over death and evil (cf. 1 John 3:1ff.).

Significantly, in this climactic outpouring of prayer, Jesus appeals to His '*Righteous Father*'.

If *Father* spelt intimate relationship, and *Holy Father*, differentness and otherness, then what does *Righteous Father* signify?

It suggests an appeal to the Fatherly God of justice who acts to reverse unjust verdicts, like the one about to be passed on the Son, and who intervenes to save from oppression and to put the world to right.

It is a prayer for His own and the Church's vindication.

As the mutual self-giving between the Persons of the Trinity is reproduced and made visible in the Church, the indifferent world will take notice and may be persuaded to acknowledge the miracle of love that only God's presence can explain.

Astonishingly, we can know ourselves loved with the same love with which the Father loves the Son!

THREE FINAL REFLECTIONS ON THE PRAYER
In the first place, the great prayer of John 17 is as much *a pre-enactment of the cross* as the foot-washing of John 13.

In the one, Jesus stoops to the mundane needs of earth; in the other, Jesus raises His eyes to the majesty of heaven.

If the foot-washing demonstrates what the cross achieves – as it were – *downwards* to our feet, the prayer shows the *upward* movement of the cross to the Father's face.

In characteristic fashion, Forsyth wrote, 'herein is prayer, not that we prayed Him, but that He first prayed us, in giving His Son to be a propitiation for us. The heart of the atonement is prayer – Christ's great self-offering to God in the Eternal Spirit.'[3]

As in praying so in dying, Christ lifts up to the Father by priestly self-offering those He has come to save. In almost every line of the prayer – with perhaps the exception of verse 9 – 'I pray for ...' could be read as 'I die for ...'

Like His prayer, His cross brings us to God and to an enjoyment of the Father's holy presence.

Like His prayer, His cross is an act of consecration by which He consecrates us to God's service.

Like His prayer, His cross sounds the defeat of evil, and pleads the ongoing protection of the Father's strong name.

The foot-washing is a silent drama to which *afterwards* meaning and proclamation will be attached. The prayer enunciates *beforehand* what the almost wordless agony of the cross will achieve. He spreads wide His arms in praying and dying to embrace all those who will 'believe in me through their word' (ESV).

So, prayerfully, the living bread casts Himself upon the deep waters of His Father's will, believing that the powerful undercurrent of love will bring Him through.

His death, like His prayer, is a doxological act, an act of worship, in which He hallows the Father's good name.

Secondly, it is likely that just as the model prayer He gave us (our Lord's Prayer) shapes the way we can pray, so here (in His

Lord's Prayer) we have *a specimen of the way He continues to pray for us from His ascended glory!*

Bearing in mind John's double angle of vision – both pre- and post-Easter – this is Andrew Lincoln's conclusion:

> Since the Jesus who prays in John 17 is also the exalted Christ, the prayer had an additional force. For it reflects the belief that even after his departure, Christ's advocacy in prayer supports the mission of his followers. Everything they have been told about their future role now has Jesus' prayer backing.[4]

Lastly, added weight is now given to our praying 'in His name'. Now that they have been made partakers of the Trinity's life, '... believers in Jesus are part of the unique prayer experience between Christ and God, and so are caught up in his intercessory praying and share in it themselves when they pray in Jesus' name'.[5]

So perhaps, to call this the high-priestly prayer of Jesus is after all, not so wide of the mark.

For fearful disciples, now as then, there can be no greater consolation than knowing that He left us this prayer as His legacy and, with it, the assurance that He prays it still.

CHAPTER SEVEN

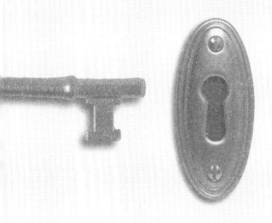

WELCOMING THE FUTURE

'Let not your hearts be troubled' (John 14:1, 27, ESV)

I saw a small boy the other day with an oversize satchel on his back waiting to cross the road to get to school. As I drove past him, I spotted his mother, at the next corner, peering round a fence, watching her son make his own way in the world.

The look on the child's face moved me to tears.

His eyes darted back to his mother, then to the potential threat from the traffic, including me, then to where he wanted to go.

I saw myself in his face.

The pale anxiety; the fearful curiosity.

I saw myself in his face not merely as I was at his age but as I am now at my age.

Can we ever be sure whether life threatens us or beckons us?

Thankfully, more often then not, the curiosity has trumped the anxiety.

I dare to believe that I have stepped through enough gaps in the traffic to make my journey worthwhile. And yet, as Vincent Van Gogh said in one of his last letters to his brother, Theo, 'the sadness never goes away'.

This itself I take to be a sign that deep down, we all want to go home.

'whatever you ask in my name …' (14:13)

In my very first weeks in Christian ministry, a longstanding church member suggested to me that surely what Jesus had said about prayer was wildly extravagant and, as a consequence, our expectations of it unrealistic.

No one, it has to be said, fathoms the gracious puzzle that is prayer.

145

All my life I have trailed along behind the memory of a father who was what used to be known as a 'prayer warrior', rising at 5 am every morning to plead through his intercessory list with great fervency. No doubt, in the mystery of such things, I am here today as a result. But I cheerfully confess that in the great prayer marathon I am right behind you!

The brutally honest among us scale down their expectations. The Christian poet, R.S. Thomas certainly did, in his poem *Folk Tales*.

> Prayers like gravel
>   Flung at the sky's
> window, hoping to attract
>   the loved one's
> attention. But without
>   visible plaits to let
> down for the believer
>   to climb up,
> to what purpose open
>   that far casement?
>   I would
> have refrained long since
>   but that peering once
> through my locked fingers
> I thought that I detected
> The movement of a curtain.[1]

This will not please the triumphalists among us. But Thomas's bleak vision is right, at least, partly so.

I am convinced that our prayers are always heard. God does not turn a deaf ear to them. I am sure that our prayers are always answered, but I am not sure that we always get answers to prayer.

Perhaps we receive something better.

If we 'abide' in Him, He tells us, we are appointed to 'bear fruit'. When we bear fruit, then we will receive whatever we ask in His name (15:16)! Surely this is an inversion of the correct order of things? Surely we pray in order that we may bear fruit? Not so, apparently. Rather we bear fruit in order to pray! This seems to imply that prayer is a means *of* grace rather than a means *to* grace.

P.T. Forsyth put the issue: 'Do we pray in order to live the Christian life? Or, do we live the Christian life in order to pray?'[2]

Certainly, in Jesus' case, John 17 is the culmination of a life already lived to the full to the glory of God.

Perhaps truly to pray 'in His name' is the 'chief end' of all our existence.

If John 17 teaches us anything about what happens when *we* pray, maybe it encourages us to believe that our praying, when joined to His praying, enters into a dialogue within the Trinity. We join a conversation, just as we join a worship, already going on.

In this sense, the curtain that veils off the holiest place has been torn away.

In which case, we do not so much pray *to* God as we pray *in* God. We do not so much pray *like* Christ, or even *with* Christ, as we pray *in* Christ.

To pray in the Spirit is to pray in the bond of love between Father and Son. Our intercession, gathered up in His intercession, places those we pray for in the loving arms of the Father and before His face.

To know this is to know that, thankfully, from time to time, the 'curtain' has twitched and we have opened our 'locked fingers' to receive His gifts.

To know this is also to gain fresh hope that one day the curtain will part completely and we shall see Him as He is.

'Walk while you have the light …' (12:35)
Throughout the writing of these reflections, I have been sustained by great music, not least that of Mozart. By turns, it was Ashkenazy or Brendel playing the piano concertos, or Elly Ameling singing the sublime *Exultate*, and much more.

Karl Barth listened to the great composer each morning in his study before beginning to write his immense *Church Dogmatics*. What the great theologian said in appreciation of Mozart and his music seems to me to capture the tone of the Farewell Discourse. Mozart, Barth suggested, heard the harmony of creation to which the shadow also belongs but in which

> the shadow is not darkness,
> deficiency is not defeat,
> sadness cannot become despair,
> trouble cannot degenerate into tragedy
> and infinite melancholy is not ultimately forced to claim
> undisputed sway …[3]

148

'... *if it were not so, I would have told you ...*' (14:2)
I have already paid my tribute to these words, but words they
remain and we stake all on believing them.

In his poem *Their Lonely Betters*, W.H. Auden muses from a
deckchair on the wordless sounds in his garden. A robin 'with no
Christian name' sings his 'Robin-Anthem' and 'rustling flowers'
wait for a passing bee.

The poet goes on,

> Not one of them was capable of lying,
> There was not one which knew that it was dying
> Or could have with a rhythm or a rhyme
> Assumed responsibility for time.

Auden concludes:

> Let them leave language to their lonely betters
> Who count some days and long for certain letters;
> We, too, make noises when we laugh and weep:
> Words are for those with promises to keep.

'*Words are for those with promises to keep.*' His words, Christ
said, are the Father's words and He speaks them as of one heart
and mind with the Father. They are the living words of the living
Word. He cannot be the Word and not keep His promise.

My life and yours, albeit by a thread, hangs on His every word.

'I am the way ... Where I am going, you cannot follow now, but you will follow later' (14:6; 13:36).

Between the departure and the arrival, there is a journey to be made. The theme of a journey or an adventure is at the heart of many of the world's great stories, from Homer's *Odyssey* to Tolkein's *Lord of the Rings*.

What makes *Lord of the Rings* a quintessentially Christian story, is that, almost uniquely in great literature, it is the story of a quest not to *gain* something but to *lose* something. For Frodo and his friends, the prize at the end is to discard the Ring.

In such a way as this, to lose one's false self in death is to gain one's true self in life and to win the whole world.

Of course, what began as a 'road less travelled' now seems, 2,000 years on, to be a well-beaten path, the salt of God's surprises trampled under the heavy foot of predictability. Only the Spirit can make the way glorious.

He does this not by making all new things but by making all things new.

He dares us to go not beyond the revelation we have received but further into it.

The Spirit therefore does not give us a mere frisson of excitement over new-fangled doctrines or heretical novelties but reconnects us to the perennial 'freshness deep down things' (Gerard Manley Hopkins) that we have already owned and loved.

Of course, Jesus is the Way in every sense.

In Lesslie Newbigin's words,

One can always travel hopefully if there is a reliable track and good ground for believing that it leads to the destination. The track on which we walk is one that disappears from sight before it reaches the destination.

We may have a vision of the peak we are aiming for, but we do not see the track all the way to it. It goes down into the dark valley of death, and we, with all our works, go that way. We can go forward with confidence because Jesus has gone that way before us and has come back from the deep valley. If He Himself is the track, we can go forward confidently even when the future is hidden. We are not lost. We have a reliable track.[4]

T.W. Manson once said that 'to follow Christ is not to go in pursuit of an ideal but to share in the results of an achievement. Christ does not ask us to go anywhere He has not already been, or do anything He has not already done.'[5]

'As you sent me into the world, I have sent them into the world. For them I sanctify myself, that they too may be truly sanctified.'
I have found these chapters of John's Gospel especially daunting. They are so rich, so deep, so unfathomable as to make me wary of a superficial treatment.

Much of the difficulty stems from the way in which the pietistic tradition from which, in part, I come, has surrounded these discourses with a mystique that is hard to penetrate.

In the hands of some interpreters, they have tended to come across as ethereal and mystical. I have been at pains to dispel this fog a little.

Not that one wants to 'dumb down' these transcendent texts: far from it. But these wonderful words must be allowed to shine their light into just that murky world of politics, economics and human frailty in which they were first spoken.

His kingdom, Jesus said, is not derived *from* this world's 'domination-system' but it is decidedly *in* it – buffeted by it and subversive of it! So although these sublime statements are *other*worldly they are not therefore *un*worldly.

All of which is to say that between gracious hospitality and glorious homecoming there is a *mission* to be accomplished.

Bruce Milne among other commentators rightly emphasises this.

What John 13–17 in turn emphasises is that mission is pre-eminently the work of the Triune God. Mission is the outgoing of the Trinity, as the Father sends the Son, and Father and Son send the Spirit. The Church is privileged to participate in the *Missio Dei*, the mission of God.

In typical fashion, Jurgen Moltmann wrote:

> In the movements of the trinitarian history of God's .dealings with the world, the church finds itself … It is not the church that has a mission of salvation to fulfil to the world; it is the mission of the Son and the Spirit through the Father that includes the church, creating a church as it goes on its way.[6]

It was part of Lesslie Newbigin's great burden to bring the *Missio Dei* to the centre of the Church's consciousness.

The great missiologist, David Bosch, concurred: 'Mission has its origin in the heart of God. God is a fountain of sending love. This is the deepest source of mission. It is impossible to penetrate deeper still; there is mission because God loves people.'[7]

And, as P.T. Forsyth said, 'God does not love us by deputy. He brings and wings his own love ... In Christ God was his own apostle.'[8]

It is a consoling thought that this same apostolic Jesus envisaged success for the mission of His future Church (John 17:20).

'I will not leave you as orphans ... I will come to you ... It is to your advantage that I go away ... I will send the Holy Spirit ...'
My parents abandoned me – when they died. I am, technically, an orphan.

I still miss them and their absence is not compensated for by the few relics they left behind: my mother's hairbrushes, my father's books, tools and old sermons; faded photo-albums each print stuck down with gummed corners ... letters in their own handwriting which cannot be thrown away.

The disciples grappled with the strange ways of God who gave His Son for the world's salvation only to take Him back so soon.

'It is to your advantage that I go away ... I will send the Spirit.'

I am not sure that the disciples at this point would have considered it a fair exchange. Yet, later, after the Spirit came, they seem to have had no regrets.

W.E. Sangster once noted that Jesus would have been only 49 years old when Paul left Antioch on his first missionary journey, and only 55 at the synod convened in Jerusalem to debate the Gentile issue.

But no one, it seems, echoed Martha's lament and said, 'If only you had been here, Lord …' Astonishingly, there is, said Sangster, 'not one word of complaint in the New Testament that Jesus Christ was no longer with His infant church'. [9]

Evidently, they felt at no disadvantage since the Spirit made Jesus real and present to them wherever they went. Yet we remain caught in the tension between His felt absence and His experienced presence.

Nowhere do we sense this tension more than at His meal – the only feature of His legacy John fails to mention explicitly. At the Lord's Table our faith is stretched between 'the night in which He was betrayed' and the 'until He come …'

Here too the secret of the Eucharist as a means of sacramental grace lies not in the material elements themselves but in the operation of the Spirit upon the actors.

As the dramatic ritual of taking, breaking, eating and drinking unfolds, the Spirit comes to meet our faith and in the synergy of grace makes known to us the Real Presence of the exalted Jesus, giving us further shares in His redeemed humanness.

Because of His absence, our experience is partial. Our knowledge falls short of certitude, postpones closure and remains open to God's future. Our faith has a deep undercurrent of listening, longing, groaning, waiting.

And, then, by the Spirit, He comes again and again. Like

Jacob, we are surprised and only in retrospect can we name the encounter.

Pierced with fierce joy, or as a hushed and holy heaviness settles on the gathering of God's people or, again, as a strange stillness and clarity freezes our religious traffic – we experience His presence with us.

Anyone who has, even for a moment, tasted the presence of God, is spoiled for lesser things and savours such experiences as foretastes of heaven.

We dare to believe Him, then, when He says that it was to our advantage that He went away.

He left us His witnesses, and nothing in all the world compares with the story they tell.

We hear His word in their words.

We have His Spirit in our hearts.

And that is enough, more than enough – at least for now!

RESOURCES

Commentaries in order of accessibility:

Bruce Milne, *The Message of John*, The Bible Speaks
Today Series (Leicester: IVP, 1993) – a fine study by a much-
loved scholar-preacher.

Gary Burge, *John, The NIV Application Commentary*
(Grand Rapids: Zondervan, 2000) – a superb example, by a
world-renowned Johannine expert, in a helpful series.

Don Carson, *The Gospel According to John* (Leicester: Inter-
Varsity Press, 1991) – a warm, theological and stimulating
study typical of Carson's work.

George Beasley-Murray, *John, Word Biblical Commentary*
(Waco: Word, 1987) – a more technical but richly insightful
exegetical study, by my own revered teacher.

Special Studies

John Pryor, *John, Evangelist of the Covenant People: The
Narrative and Themes of the Fourth Gospel* (London: Darton,
Longman & Todd, 1992). A fascinating and very helpful
exercise in biblical theology.

Andrew T. Lincoln, *Truth on Trial: The Lawsuit Motif in the Fourth Gospel* (Peabody: Hendrickson, 2000) – a fascinating exploration of one aspect of John's vision which marvellously opened up the whole Gospel for me.

'God's Name, Jesus' Name and Prayer in the Fourth Gospel', in ed. Richard Longenecker, *Into God's Presence; Prayer in the New Testament* (Grand Rapids: Eerdmans, 2001) – especially helpful on John 17.

Craig Koester, *Symbolism in the Fourth Gospel: Meaning, Mystery, Community* (Minneapolis: Fortress Press, 2003) – a unique and illuminating book that helped me immensely.

Anthony Kelly and Francis Moloney, *Experiencing God in the Gospel of John* (New York: Paulist Press, 2003) – a rich, theological, Catholic exposition of John, full of wonderful insights and moving devotional writing.

NOTES

Chapter 1

1. Ray Bradbury, 'In a Season of Calm Weather' in *The Day it Rained Forever* (London: The Science Fiction Book Club, 1960) p.31. I have taken a great risk in seeking to summarise this short story by a brilliant writer. I urge you to read Bradbury firsthand.
2. John Pryor, *John, The Evangelist of the Covenant People: The Narrative and Themes of the Fourth Gospel* (Darton, Longman and Todd, 1992) p.58.
3. G.R. Beasley-Murray, *John, Word Biblical Commentary* (Waco: Word, 1987) p.212.
4. D.A. Carson, *The Gospel According to John* (Leicester: Inter-Varsity Press, 1991) p.440.
5. P.T. Forsyth, *The Justification of God* (London: Independent Press, 1917/1948) p.221.
6. I have drawn heavily here on Andrew T. Lincoln, *Truth on Trial: The Lawsuit Motif in the Fourth Gospel* (Peabody: Hendrickson, 2000).
7. A.M. Ramsey, *The Glory of God and the Transfiguration of Christ* (London: Longman, Green and Co, 1949) p.81.
8. Lincoln, *Truth on Trial*, op. cit. pp.244–5.

Chapter 2

1. Anthony Kelly and Francis Maloney, *Experiencing God in the Gospel of John* (New York: Paulist Press, 2003) p.271.
2. Bruce Milne, *The Message of John, the Bible Speaks Today* series (Leicester: InterVarsity Press, 1993) p.197.
3. Craig Koester, *Symbolism in the Fourth Gospel: Meaning, Mystery, Community* (Minneapolis: Fortress Press, 2003) p.11.
4. Hans Boersma, *Violence, Hospitality, and the Cross* (Grand Rapids: Baker Books, 2004) p.15.
5. Jonathan Wilson, *Gospel Virtues* (Downers Grove: IVP, 1998) p.172.
6. Koester, *Symbolism*, op. cit. p.133.
7. Andrew T. Lincoln, 'Power, Judgment, and Possession: John's Gospel in Political Perspective' in Craig Bartholomew, Jonathan Caplin, Robert Song, Al Wolters, (eds.) *A Royal Priesthood: The Use of the*

Bible Ethically and Politically: A Dialogue with Oliver O'Donovan (Carlisle: Paternoster, 2002) p.162.

8. Kelly and Moloney, *Experiencing God in the Gospel of John*, op. cit. pp.287, 285.

9. Boersma, *Violence, Hospitality and the Cross*, op. cit. p.16.

10. Michael J. Gorman, *Cruciformity: Paul's Narrative Spirituality of the Cross* (Grand Rapids: Eerdmans, 2001) p.246.

11. Reinhard Hutter, 'The Disclosure of Practices in Worship and Theology' in Miroslav Wolf and Dorothy Bass (eds.), *Practising Theology: Beliefs and Practices in Christian Life* (Grand Rapids: Eerdmans, 2002) p.219.

12. Wilson, *Gospel Virtues*, op. cit. p.171.

13. See Henri Nouwen, *Reaching Out: The Three Movements of the Spiritual Life* (Glasgow: Fount, 1980).

14. David Ford, *The Shape of Living* (Grand Rapids: Baker, 1997) p.32.

15. Douglas D. Webster, *A Passion for Christ: An Evangelical Christology* (Grand Rapids: Zondervan, 1987) p.55. I keep returning to this brilliant book.

16. Gordon Wakefield, *The Liturgy of St. John* (London: Epworth Press, 1985) p.25.

17. Kelly and Moloney, *Experiencing God in the Gospel of John* op. cit. p.283.

18. See Don Carson, *Love in Hard Places* (Carlisle: Paternoster, 2002) pp.12–13, 30ff.; and further in *Exegetical Fallacies*, 2nd edition (Downers Grove: IVP, 1997) Chapter 8.

19. Ibid. p.61.

20. Carson, *The Gospel According to John*, op. cit. p.486.

21. Lewis B. Smedes, *Standing on the Promises: Keeping Hope Alive for a Tomorrow We Cannot Control* (Nashville: Nelson, 1998) p.173.

Chapter 3

1. Gary Burge, *John: The NIV Application Commentary* (Grand Rapids: Zondervan, 2000) p.397.

2. Smedes, *Standing on the Promises*, op. cit. p.124.

3. Kelly and Moloney, *Experiencing God in the Gospel of John*, op. cit. p.291.

4. There is much more that might be said on this topic; I have only pointed the way. See further the crucial work Chris Wright has

done in linking the Oneness of Yahweh in the Old Testament to the uniqueness of Jesus.

For example: Wright's contribution to the essays collected in Bruce Nicholls (ed.), *The Unique Christ in Our Pluralist World*, (Carlisle: Paternoster, 1994).

See also Chris Wright, *Thinking Clearly about the Uniqueness of Jesus* (Crowborough: Monarch, 1997); also Wright's article in another very useful symposium, Andrew Clarke and Bruce Winter (eds.), *One God, One Lord: Christianity in a World of Religious Pluralism*, (Grand Rapids: Baker Books, 1992).

5. David M. Ball in the symposium mentioned in the previous note, at p.79.
6. Koester, *Symbolism in the Fourth Gospel*, op. cit. p.298.
7. Burge, *John*, op. cit. p.403.
8. George Hunsberger, 'Missional Vocation: Called and Sent to Represent the Reign of God' in Darrell Guder (ed.), *Missional Church: A Vision for the Sending of the Church in North America* (Grand Rapids: Eerdmans, 1998) pp.106–7.
9. Burge, *John*, op. cit. pp.394–5.
10. Kelly and Moloney, *Experiencing God in the Gospel of John*, op. cit. p.294.
11. Gordon Fee, *God's Empowering Presence: The Holy Spirit in the Letters of Paul* (Peabody: Hendrickson, 1994) p.715.
12. Tom Smail, *The Giving Gift: The Holy Spirit in Person* (London: Hodder, 1988) p.35.
13. J.I. Packer, *Keep in Step with the Spirit* (Leicester: IVP, 1984) p.47.
14. Andrew T. Lincoln, *Truth on Trial: The Lawsuit Motif in the Fourth Gospel* (Peabody: Hendrickson, 2000) p.111.
15. Kelly and Moloney, *Experiencing God in the Gospel of John*, op. cit. p.296.
16. Walter Wink, *Engaging the Powers: Discernment and Resistance in a World of Domination* (Minneapolis: Fortress Press, 1992) p.51.
17. Ibid. p.53.
18. Austin Farrer, *A Faith of Our Own* (Cleveland: The World Publishing Co. 1960) p.132.
19. Samuel Chadwick (ed.), *The Way to Pentecost* (London: Hodder, 1951) p.43.

20. Lincoln, *Truth on Trial*, op. cit. p.111.
21. W.E. Sangster, *The Pure in Heart* (London: Epworth Press, 1957) p.119.

Chapter 4

1. Abraham Heschel, *Moral Grandeur and Spiritual Audacity*, Susannah Heschel (ed.), (New York: Farrar, Strause, and Giroux, 1996) p.10.
2. Koester, *Symbolism in the Fourth Gospel*, p.274.
3. Burge, *John*, op.cit. pp.424–5.
4. Quoted in John Piper, *The Legacy of Sovereign Joy: God's Triumphant Grace in the Lives of Augustine, Luther, and Calvin* (Leicester: InterVarsity Press, 2000), p.57.
5. Ibid. p.74.
6. Ibid. p.431.
7. Ibid. p.432.
8. For an extended popular exposition of this theme, exploring its current political implications, together with moving pen-portraits of contemporary Palestinian Christians, I strongly recommend Gary Burge's recently revised and re-issued book: *Whose Land? Whose Promise? What Christians Are Not Being Told About Israel and the Palestinians* (Carlisle: Paternoster, 2003).
9. Lesslie Newbigin, *The Light Has Come: An Exposition of the Fourth Gospel* (Grand Rapids: Eerdmans, 1982) p.202.
10. Milne, *John*, op. cit. p.223.
11. Koester, *Symbolism in the Fourth Gospel*, op. cit. p.268.
12. Kelly and Moloney, *Experiencing God in the Gospel of John*, op. cit. p.312.
13. Quoted in Milne, *John*, op. cit. p.225.

Chapter 5

1. Kelly and Moloney, *Experiencing God in the Gospel of John*, op. cit. p.296.
2. Milne, *John*, op. cit. p.229.
3. Ibid. p.229.
4. Kelly and Moloney, op.cit. p.319.
5. J.H. Bavinck, *An Introduction to the Science of Missions* (Philadelphia: Presbyterian and Reformed Publishing Co. 1964) pp.260–1.
6. Lincoln, *Truth on Trial*, op. cit. p.119.

7. Koester, *Symbolism in the Fourth Gospel*, op. cit. p.281.
8. John Taylor, *The Go-Between God: The Holy Spirit and the Christian Mission* (London: SCM Press, 1972) p.19.
9. Packer, *Keep in Step with the Spirit*, op. cit. p.66.
10. Farrer, *A Faith of Our Own*, op. cit. p.34.
11. P.T. Forsyth, *The Justification of God*, op. cit. p.221.
12. Ibid. pp.218–9.
13. Newbigin, *The Light Has Come*, op. cit. p.222.

Chapter 6
1. Carson, *The Gospel According to John*, op. cit. p.567.
2. Milne, *John*, op. cit. pp.237–8.
3. P.T. Forsyth, *The Soul of Prayer* (London: Epworth Press, 1916) p.15.
4. Lincoln, 'God's Name, Jesus' Name and Prayer in the Fourth Gospel', op. cit. p.171.
5. Ibid. p.171.

Chapter 7
1. R.S. Thomas, *Collected Poems, 1945–1990* (London: JM Dent, a division of The Orion Publishing Group, 1995).
2. P.T. Forsyth, *The Soul of Prayer*, op. cit. p.18.
3. Karl Barth, *Theologian of Freedom: Selected Writings*, Clifford Green (ed.), (London: Collins, n.d.) p.323.
4. Lesslie Newbigin, *The Gospel in a Pluralist Society* (London: SPCK, 1989) p.115.
5. T.W. Manson, *Ethics and the Gospel* (London: SCM Press, 1962) p.59.
6. Jurgen Moltmann, *The Church in the Power of the Spirit* (London: SCM Press, 1977) p.64.
7. David J. Bosch, *Transforming Mission: Paradigm Shifts in Theology of Mission* (Maryknoll, NewYork: Orbis Books, 1991) p.392.
8. P.T. Forsyth, *Revelation, Old and New* (London: Independent Press, 1962) p.11.
9. W.E. Sangster, *Why Jesus Never Wrote A Book* (London: Epworth Press, 1956) p.69.

NATIONAL DISTRIBUTORS

UK: (and countries not listed below)
CWR, Waverley Abbey House, Waverley Lane, Farnham, Surrey GU9 8EP.
Tel: (01252) 784700 Outside UK +44 1252 784700

AUSTRALIA: CMC Australasia, PO Box 519, Belmont, Victoria 3216.
Tel: (03) 5241 3288

CANADA: Cook Communications Ministries, PO Box 98, 55 Woodslee Avenue, Paris, Ontario.
Tel: 1800 263 2664

GHANA: Challenge Enterprises of Ghana, PO Box 5723, Accra.
Tel: (021) 222437/223249 Fax: (021) 226227

HONG KONG: Cross Communications Ltd, 1/F, 562A Nathan Road, Kowloon.
Tel: 2780 1188 Fax: 2770 6229

INDIA: Crystal Communications, 10-3-18/4/1, East Marredpalli, Secunderabad – 500026,
Andhra Pradesh.
Tel/Fax: (040) 27737145

KENYA: Keswick Books and Gifts Ltd, PO Box 10242, Nairobi.
Tel: (02) 331692/226047 Fax: (02) 728557

MALAYSIA: Salvation Book Centre (M) Sdn Bhd, 23 Jalan SS 2/64, 47300 Petaling Jaya, Selangor.
Tel: (03) 78766411/78766797 Fax: (03) 78757066/78756360

NEW ZEALAND: CMC Australasia, PO Box 36015, Lower Hutt.
Tel: 0800 449 408 Fax: 0800 449 049

NIGERIA: FBFM, Helen Baugh House, 96 St Finbarr's College Road, Akoka, Lagos.
Tel: (01) 7747429/4700218/825775/827264

PHILIPPINES: OMF Literature Inc, 776 Boni Avenue, Mandaluyong City.
Tel: (02) 531 2183 Fax: (02) 531 1960

SINGAPORE: Armour Publishing Pte Ltd, Block 203A Henderson Road,
11–06 Henderson Industrial Park, Singapore 159546.
Tel: 6 276 9976 Fax: 6 276 7564

SOUTH AFRICA: Struik Christian Books, 80 MacKenzie Street, PO Box 1144, Cape Town 8000.
Tel: (021) 462 4360 Fax: (021) 461 3612

SRI LANKA: Christombu Books, 27 Hospital Street, Colombo 1.
Tel: (01) 433142/328909

TANZANIA: CLC Christian Book Centre, PO Box 1384, Mkwepu Street, Dar es Salaam.
Tel/Fax: (022) 2119439

USA: Cook Communications Ministries, PO Box 98, 55 Woodslee Avenue, Paris, Ontario, Canada.
Tel: 1800 263 2664

ZIMBABWE: Word of Life Books, Shop 4, Memorial Building, 35 S Machel Avenue, Harare.
Tel: (04) 781305 Fax: (04) 774739

For email addresses, visit the CWR website: www.cwr.org.uk

CWR is a registered charity – number 294387

Day and Residential Courses
Counselling Training
Leadership Development
Biblical Study Courses
Regional Seminars
Ministry to Women
Daily Devotionals
Books and Videos
Conference Centre

Trusted all Over the World

CWR HAS GAINED A WORLDWIDE reputation as a centre of excellence for Bible-based training and resources. From our headquarters at Waverley Abbey House, Farnham, England, we have been serving God's people for 40 years with a vision to help apply God's Word to everyday life and relationships. The daily devotional *Every Day with Jesus* is read by nearly a million readers an issue in more than 150 countries, and our unique courses in biblical studies and pastoral care are respected all over the world. Waverley Abbey House provides a conference centre in a tranquil setting.

For free brochures on our seminars and courses, conference facilities, or a catalogue of CWR resources, please contact us at the following address.
CWR, Waverley Abbey House, Waverley Lane, Farnham, Surrey GU9 8EP, UK

Telephone: +44 (0)1252 784700
Email: mail@cwr.org.uk
Website: www.cwr.org.uk

God's Questions
Philip Greenslade

Philip Greenslade brings a unique perspective to familiar Bible passages, revealing hidden truths and life-changing applications. He challenges you to listen to the questions God first asked man and apply them to your own life:

• Where are you in your relationship with God?
• Who told you how to understand and what you know?
• What is this that you have done – do you take responsibility?
• Why are you angry – how do you deal with life and emotions?
• Where is your brother – how do you relate to others?

£6.99 (plus p&p)
ISBN: 1-85345-259-9

Price correct at time of printing